PostgreSQL 15 Cookbook

100+ expert solutions across scalability, performance optimization, essential commands, cloud provisioning, backup, and recovery

Peter G

Published by: GitforGits
Publisher: Sonal Dhandre
www.gitforgits.com
support@gitforgits.com

Printed in India

First Printing: March 2023

ISBN: 978-8119177059

Cover Design by: Kitten Publishing

For permission to use material from this book, please contact GitforGits at support@GitforGits.com.

Content

Preface

If you're a PostgreSQL database administrator looking for a comprehensive guide to managing your databases, look no further than the PostgreSQL 15 Cookbook. With 100 ready solutions to common database management challenges, this book provides a complete guide to administering and troubleshooting your databases.

Starting with cloud provisioning and migration, the book covers all aspects of database administration, including replication, transaction logs, partitioning, sharding, auditing, realtime monitoring, backup, recovery, and error debugging. Each solution is presented in a clear, easy-to-follow format, using a real database called 'adventureworks' to provide an on-job practicing experience.

Throughout the book, you'll learn how to use tools like pglogical, pgloader, WAL, repmgr, Patroni, HAProxy, PgBouncer, pgBackRest, pgAudit and Prometheus, gaining valuable experience and expertise in managing your databases.

With its focus on practical solutions and real-world scenarios, the PostgreSQL 15 Cookbook is an essential resource for any PostgreSQL database administrator. Whether you're just starting out or you're a seasoned pro, this book has everything you need to keep your databases running smoothly and efficiently.

In this book you will learn how to:

- Streamline your PostgreSQL databases with cloud provisioning and migration techniques
- Optimize performance and scalability through effective replication, partitioning, and sharding
- Safeguard your databases with robust auditing, backup, and recovery strategies
- Monitor your databases in real-time with powerful tools like pgAudit, Prometheus, and Patroni
- Troubleshoot errors and debug your databases with expert techniques and best practices
- Boost your productivity and efficiency with advanced tools like pglogical, pgloader, and HAProxy.

With the PostgreSQL 15 Cookbook as your guide, you'll gain valuable insights and expertise in managing your PostgreSQL databases, while learning practical solutions to common database management challenges. Whether you're a novice or an experienced

PostgreSQL administrator, this book has everything you need to take your database management skills to the next level and become a PostgreSQL expert.

GitforGits

Prerequisites

This book is ideal for database administrators, developers, and IT professionals who are responsible for managing and troubleshooting PostgreSQL databases. It is also suitable for beginners looking to learn more about PostgreSQL administration and best practices.

Codes Usage

Are you in need of some helpful code examples to assist you in your programming and documentation? Look no further! Our book offers a wealth of supplemental material, including code examples and exercises.

Not only is this book here to aid you in getting your job done, but you have our permission to use the example code in your programs and documentation. However, please note that if you are reproducing a significant portion of the code, we do require you to contact us for permission.

But don't worry, using several chunks of code from this book in your program or answering a question by citing our book and quoting example code does not require permission. But if you do choose to give credit, an attribution typically includes the title, author, publisher, and ISBN. For example, "PostgreSQL 15 Cookbook by Peter G".

If you are unsure whether your intended use of the code examples falls under fair use or the permissions outlined above, please do not hesitate to reach out to us at kittenpub.kdp@gmail.com.

We are happy to assist and clarify any concerns.

Acknowledgement

I would like to express my deep gratitude to GitforGits, for their unwavering support and guidance throughout the writing of this book. Their expertise and attention to detail helped to ensure that the content was accurate, informative, and accessible to readers of all levels of expertise. Their contributions, from copyediting and design to marketing and promotion, have been invaluable in making this book a success.

Finally, I would like to thank my family and friends for their love and support, which has been a constant source of inspiration throughout this journey. Writing this book would not have been possible without their encouragement and encouragement.

Thank you all for your contributions to this project, and for your ongoing support of my work.

Chapter 1: Getting PostgreSQL 15 Ready

Recipe#1: Simplifying Understanding of PostgreSQL Architecture

PostgreSQL is a powerful, open-source database management system that is widely used in applications that require efficient and reliable data storage and retrieval. PostgreSQL is an object-relational database management system (ORDBMS), which means that it is designed to store and retrieve data using an object-oriented approach while also supporting the relational database model.

The PostgreSQL architecture is built around a client-server model, with the PostgreSQL server process at the center. The server process is responsible for handling all database requests from clients, and it communicates with clients using the PostgreSQL network protocol. Clients can connect to the server process using various methods, including a command-line interface (CLI), graphical user interface (GUI), or application programming interface (API).

In addition to the server process, the PostgreSQL architecture includes several auxiliary processes that work together to ensure efficient and reliable data storage and retrieval. These processes include the background writer, the checkpoint process, the autovacuum process, and the write-ahead log (WAL) writer process.

The background writer is responsible for writing modified data from memory to disk, while the checkpoint process ensures that the data on disk is consistent with the current state of the database. The autovacuum process is responsible for cleaning up dead rows in the database, and the WAL writer process is responsible for managing transaction logs.

PostgreSQL stores data in databases, which are composed of several objects, including tables, indexes, sequences, and views. Tables are used to store data, while indexes are used to improve the performance of data retrieval. Sequences are used to generate unique values, and views are used to provide a customized view of data to clients.

PostgreSQL also supports various data types, including numeric, text, date/time, and Boolean. This flexibility allows developers to build applications that can handle a wide range of data types and formats.

Overall, the PostgreSQL architecture is designed to provide efficient and reliable data storage and retrieval in a wide range of applications. Its client-server model, auxiliary processes, and support for various data types make it a versatile and powerful database management system.

Recipe#2: Installing PostgreSQL 15 from Binaries

To install PostgreSQL 15 from binaries on a Linux machine, follow these steps:

- Download the PostgreSQL 15 binaries for your Linux distribution from the PostgreSQL download page.

- Extract the downloaded archive to a directory of your choice.

- Create a new system user to run the PostgreSQL service:

```
sudo adduser postgres
```

- Change to the extracted directory and run the installation script:

```
cd postgresql-15.x.y
sudo ./configure
sudo make
sudo make install
```

- Initialize the PostgreSQL database cluster:

```
sudo su - postgres
initdb -D /usr/local/pgsql/data
exit
```

- Start the PostgreSQL service:

```
sudo systemctl start postgresql
```

You can now connect to the PostgreSQL server using the psql command-line utility.

Recipe#3: Installing PostgreSQL 15 from Source Code

To install PostgreSQL 15 from source code on a Linux machine, follow these steps:

- Download the PostgreSQL 15 source code from the PostgreSQL download page.

- Extract the downloaded archive to a directory of your choice.

- Install the required dependencies:

```
sudo apt-get install build-essential libreadline-dev zlib1g-dev flex bison
```

- Change to the extracted directory and run the configuration script:

```
cd postgresql-15.x.y
./configure
```

- Compile and install PostgreSQL:

```
make
sudo make install
```

- Initialize the PostgreSQL database cluster:

```
sudo su - postgres
initdb -D /usr/local/pgsql/data
exit
```

- Start the PostgreSQL service:

```
sudo systemctl start postgresql
```

You can now connect to the PostgreSQL server using the psql command-line utility.

Recipe#4: Upgrade to Minor & Major Releases

To upgrade to a minor release of PostgreSQL (e.g., from version 15.1 to 15.2), follow these steps:

- Download the new PostgreSQL binaries for your system from the PostgreSQL download page.

- Stop the PostgreSQL service:

```
sudo systemctl stop postgresql
```

- Extract the downloaded archive to a temporary directory.

- Replace the existing PostgreSQL binaries with the new ones:

```
sudo cp -R new_postgresql_directory /usr/local/pgsql/
```

- Restart the PostgreSQL service:

```
sudo systemctl start postgresql
```

To upgrade to a major release of PostgreSQL (e.g., from version 14 to version 15), follow these steps:

- Create a backup of your existing PostgreSQL database:

```
pg_dumpall > backup.sql
```

- Stop the PostgreSQL service:

```
sudo systemctl stop postgresql
```

- Download and install the new version of PostgreSQL using the installation method of your choice.

- Upgrade the existing PostgreSQL database:

```
sudo pg_upgrade -b /usr/local/pgsql/14/bin -B /usr/local/pgsql/15/bin -d /usr/local/pgsql/14/data -D /usr/local/pgsql/15/data
```

- Start the PostgreSQL service:

```
sudo systemctl start postgresql
```

- Verify the upgrade was successful by connecting to the new version of PostgreSQL and checking that your data is intact.

Recipe#5: Parsing Database Start-up Logs

The PostgreSQL server logs various messages during start-up, including information about the server version, database configuration, and startup process. To parse these logs, follow these steps:

- Locate the PostgreSQL log files. By default, PostgreSQL logs to the pg_log subdirectory of the data directory.

- Open the log file using a text editor or command-line utility.

- Look for lines that start with a timestamp, such as:

```
2023-03-22 12:34:56.789 EDT [12345] LOG:  database system is ready to accept connections
```

- Use the timestamp to identify the sequence of events during the server startup process.

- Look for lines that contain error messages or warnings, such as:

```
2023-03-22 12:34:56.789 EDT [12345] ERROR:  relation "table_name" does not exist
```

- Use the error message to identify and troubleshoot any issues that occurred during the server startup process.

Recipe#6: Using PostgreSQL Server Access Solutions

PostgreSQL provides several server access solutions, including the following:
- Command-line interface (CLI): PostgreSQL provides a command-line utility called psql that allows you to connect to a PostgreSQL server and execute SQL commands.
- Graphical user interface (GUI): Several GUI tools are available for PostgreSQL, including pgAdmin and DBeaver. These tools provide a visual interface for managing databases and executing SQL commands.
- Application programming interface (API): PostgreSQL provides several APIs for interacting with the server programmatically, including libpq and JDBC.

To use these server access solutions, follow these steps:
- Install the desired server access solution on your system.
- Configure the connection settings for the PostgreSQL server, including the server address, port number, and authentication credentials.
- Connect to the PostgreSQL server using the selected access solution.
- Use the access solution to execute SQL commands, manage databases and database objects, and monitor server activity.

Recipe#7: Discovering PostgreSQL Database Structural Objects

PostgreSQL databases are composed of several structural objects, including tables, indexes, sequences, views, and stored procedures.

To discover these objects, follow these steps:
- Connect to the PostgreSQL server using a server access solution, such as psql.
- List the available databases using the \l command.
- Select the database of interest using the \c command.
- List the available schema using the \dn command.
- Select the schema of interest using the SET search_path command.
- List the available objects in the selected schema using the \dt, \di, \ds, and \df commands.
- Use the available commands and documentation to explore the available objects and their properties.

Recipe#8:   Understanding   PostgreSQL Memory Configuration

PostgreSQL uses memory in several ways, including for caching data and executing queries. To configure memory usage in PostgreSQL, follow these steps:

- Determine the available system memory and the expected workload for the PostgreSQL server.
- Configure the following memory-related parameters in the postgresql.conf configuration file:
    - shared_buffers: This parameter specifies the amount of memory allocated for shared memory buffers used for caching data. The default value is typically 25% of the available system memory.
    - work_mem: This parameter specifies the amount of memory allocated for each worker process used for sorting and hashing. The default value is typically 4MB.
    - maintenance_work_mem: This parameter specifies the amount of memory allocated for maintenance tasks, such as vacuuming and indexing. The default value is typically 64MB.
    - max_connections: This parameter specifies the maximum number of concurrent connections allowed to the server. The default value is typically 100.
- Monitor memory usage and adjust the configuration parameters as needed to optimize performance and avoid resource exhaustion.

Recipe#9:   Understanding   Use   of   Key Configuration Parameters

PostgreSQL provides several configuration parameters that can be adjusted to optimize performance and functionality. Some of the key parameters and their advantages are listed below:

- shared_buffers: This parameter specifies the amount of memory allocated for shared memory buffers used for caching data. Increasing this value can improve read performance by reducing the frequency of disk reads.
- work_mem: This parameter specifies the amount of memory allocated for each worker process used for sorting and hashing. Increasing this value can improve query performance by allowing more data to be sorted or hashed in memory.
- maintenance_work_mem: This parameter specifies the amount of memory

allocated for maintenance tasks, such as vacuuming and indexing. Increasing this value can improve maintenance performance by allowing more data to be processed in memory.

- max_connections: This parameter specifies the maximum number of concurrent connections allowed to the server. Increasing this value can improve scalability by allowing more clients to connect to the server simultaneously.
- effective_cache_size: This parameter specifies the estimated size of the operating system's disk cache. Adjusting this value can help the query planner make better decisions about query execution plans by providing a more accurate estimate of the available cache.
- autovacuum: This parameter specifies whether automatic vacuuming of tables and indexes should be performed. Enabling this parameter can help maintain database performance by cleaning up dead rows and improving index efficiency.
- checkpoint_timeout: This parameter specifies the frequency at which checkpoints are performed. Adjusting this value can help balance the trade-off between recovery time and server performance by reducing the amount of data that needs to be recovered after a crash.
- checkpoint_completion_target: This parameter specifies the amount of time that a checkpoint should take as a fraction of the checkpoint_timeout value. Adjusting this value can help optimize server performance by balancing the trade-off between checkpoint frequency and checkpoint overhead.
- effective_io_concurrency: This parameter specifies the number of concurrent I/O operations that can be performed on the server. Adjusting this value can help optimize server performance by allowing the server to perform more I/O operations in parallel.
- max_wal_size: This parameter specifies the maximum size of the write-ahead log (WAL) files. Adjusting this value can help optimize server performance by balancing the trade-off between WAL size and recovery time after a crash.
- temp_buffers: This parameter specifies the amount of memory allocated for temporary data used in sorting and hashing. Increasing this value can improve query performance by allowing more data to be sorted or hashed in memory.
- random_page_cost: This parameter specifies the estimated cost of a random page access. Adjusting this value can help the query planner make better decisions about query execution plans by providing a more accurate estimate of the cost of random I/O operations.
- seq_page_cost: This parameter specifies the estimated cost of a sequential page access. Adjusting this value can help the query planner make better decisions about query execution plans by providing a more accurate estimate of the cost of sequential I/O operations.
- max_worker_processes: This parameter specifies the maximum number of background worker processes that can be spawned by the server. Increasing this

value can help improve scalability by allowing more background processes to be used for maintenance and other tasks.

By adjusting these parameters based on your system requirements and workload, you can optimize the performance and functionality of your PostgreSQL server.

It is important to note that changing these configuration parameters can have both positive and negative effects on your PostgreSQL server's performance and stability. Therefore, it is important to carefully test and monitor your server after making any changes to these parameters to ensure that they have the desired effect.

In addition to the configuration parameters listed above, PostgreSQL also provides a wide range of other parameters that can be used to customize the behavior of the server. These parameters are documented in the PostgreSQL documentation and can be adjusted as needed to meet your specific requirements.

Overall, understanding the key configuration parameters in PostgreSQL and how they affect server performance and functionality is an important aspect of database administration. By carefully configuring and monitoring your PostgreSQL server, you can ensure that it provides reliable, efficient, and high-performance data storage and retrieval for your applications.

CHAPTER 2: PERFORMING BASIC POSTGRESQL OPERATIONS

Recipe#1: Understanding AdventureWorks Database in this Book

The AdventureWorks database, is accessible through the below link: https://github.com/kittenpub/database-repository/blob/main/data.zip

This database is an open-source PostgreSQL sample database designed as a learning tool for database professionals and application developers. This comprehensive database contains information about various aspects of a fictitious bicycle and accessories manufacturing company called Adventure Works Cycles. It contains numerous tables, views, stored procedures, and other database objects that help simulate real-world business scenarios. The AdventureWorks database serves as an ideal resource in this book for understanding how to design, develop, and manage complex database structures and applications using PostgreSQL 15.

The AdventureWorks database is organized into several schemas to facilitate better organization and management of database objects. The schemas include:

- Production: This schema encompasses the manufacturing and production process, including information about products, product categories, product models, work orders, and bill of materials. It also contains data about product descriptions, manufacturing steps, and product inventory.

- Sales: The Sales schema is responsible for tracking sales-related information, such as customers, sales orders, sales order details, sales territories, and salespersons. It also manages shipping and billing addresses, as well as special offers and discounts.

- Purchasing: The Purchasing schema deals with the procurement process for raw materials and components required for production. It includes information about vendors, purchase orders, purchase order details, and vendor contacts.

- HumanResources: This schema manages employee-related data such as employee information, job titles, pay structures, and departmental hierarchies. It also handles data on employee shifts and attendance.

- Person: The Person schema centralizes data about people involved with the company, including employees, customers, vendors, and contacts. It stores personal details such as names, addresses, email addresses, and phone numbers.

- dbo: The dbo schema contains a set of miscellaneous database objects that do not belong to any specific business area or schema.

The AdventureWorks database enables users to practice various database tasks and operations, such as creating and altering tables, building relationships between tables, writing SQL queries, designing and implementing stored procedures, triggers, and views, and performing performance optimizations. It also serves as a useful resource for understanding database normalization and the principles of good database design.

The tables within the AdventureWorks database are designed to simulate realistic business scenarios, with primary and foreign key relationships, indexes, and constraints. The data is carefully crafted to demonstrate the complexities and intricacies of real-world business processes.

To further enhance the learning experience, the AdventureWorks database also includes a set of pre-defined views that can be used to simplify complex queries and retrieve data efficiently. These views cover various aspects of the business, such as sales summary, production details, and customer information. Additionally, there are stored procedures and functions to demonstrate the use of procedural programming within the database.

Recipe#2: Selecting Right Database Schema

PostgreSQL is a powerful relational database management system (RDBMS) that allows you to organize your data using schemas. A schema is a logical container that groups together related database objects such as tables, views, indexes, and sequences. This helps to organize the database, making it more manageable and easier to maintain. In this recipe, we will discuss in detail the concept of defining PostgreSQL schemas, their types, and how to create them.

PostgreSQL Schema Types

PostgreSQL supports two types of schemas, Public and Private.
- Public Schema: Public schema is the default schema created by PostgreSQL. When a new database is created, all the objects are automatically created in the public schema. This schema is accessible to all users who have access to the database.
- Private Schema: A private schema is created by a user and can only be accessed by that user or other users who have been granted explicit permission. Private schemas allow users to organize their objects and data, limiting access to them for security reasons.

Creating Schema

To create a new schema, use the CREATE SCHEMA command, followed by the name of the new schema:

CREATE SCHEMA sales;

This will create a new schema called "sales". By default, the schema will be created in the current database's search path.

You can also specify the owner of the schema using the AUTHORIZATION clause:

CREATE SCHEMA sales AUTHORIZATION sales_user;

This command creates a new schema called "sales" and sets "sales_user" as the owner of the schema.

Moving Object to Different Schema

To move an object to a different schema, use the ALTER SCHEMA command, followed by the object you want to move and the new schema:

ALTER TABLE sales.orders SET SCHEMA sales;

This command moves the "orders" table from the "sales" schema to the "orders" schema.

Benefits of Using PostgreSQL Schema

Organizing database objects into schemas can provide many benefits, including:
- Improved Manageability: Schemas help to organize database objects into logical groups based on their function or purpose. This makes it easier to manage and maintain the database.
- Enhanced Security: Private schemas allow users to limit access to their objects and data, improving security.
- Easier Collaboration: Schemas can help teams collaborate more effectively by providing a clear organization structure for their database objects.
- Better Performance: By organizing database objects into schemas, you can optimize database performance by reducing the number of queries needed to retrieve data.

Defining PostgreSQL schemas is a crucial part of database management that allows you to logically group related database objects together. Schemas provide many benefits, including improved manageability, enhanced security, and better performance. By following the steps outlined in this recipe, you can create, move, and manage schemas in PostgreSQL, making your database more organized and easier to maintain.

Recipe#3: Selecting Indexing Techniques

Indexing is a crucial aspect of database optimization that helps to speed up queries by creating a separate data structure that points to the location of data in a table. PostgreSQL offers various indexing techniques that can be used to improve database performance. In this recipe, we will discuss the different indexing techniques supported by PostgreSQL and how they can be used to optimize database queries.

Indexing Techniques in PostgreSQL

PostgreSQL supports the following indexing techniques:

- B-tree Indexing: This is the default indexing technique used in PostgreSQL. It is used to index data that can be sorted in a particular order, such as numbers or text. B-tree indexing is efficient for range queries, such as finding values within a specific range. To create a B-tree index in PostgreSQL, use the following command:

```
CREATE INDEX idx_order_id ON sales.orders(order_id);
```

This creates a B-tree index on the "order_id" column in the "orders" table.

- Hash Indexing: Hash indexing is used to index data that can be hashed, such as integer values. Hash indexing is faster than B-tree indexing for equality comparisons but slower for range queries. To create a hash index in PostgreSQL, use the following command:

```
CREATE INDEX idx_customer_id ON sales.customers USING HASH (customer_id);
```

This creates a hash index on the "customer_id" column in the "customers" table.

- GiST Indexing: GiST stands for Generalized Search Tree, and it is used for complex data types such as geometric shapes or text documents. GiST allows custom search algorithms to be used for indexing. To create a GiST index in PostgreSQL, use the following command:

CREATE INDEX idx_product_geom ON production.products USING GiST (geom);

This creates a GiST index on the "geom" column in the "products" table.

- SP-GiST Indexing: SP-GiST stands for Space-Partitioned Generalized Search Tree, and it is used for indexing spatial data or other complex data types. To create an SP-GiST index in PostgreSQL, use the following command:

CREATE INDEX idx_product_geom ON production.products USING SPGIST (geom);

This creates an SP-GiST index on the "geom" column in the "products" table.

- GIN Indexing: GIN stands for Generalized Inverted Index, and it is used for indexing array data types or full-text search. To create a GIN index in PostgreSQL, use the following command:

CREATE INDEX idx_product_tags ON production.products USING GIN (tags);

This creates a GIN index on the "tags" column in the "products" table.

- BRIN Indexing: BRIN stands for Block Range INdex, and it is used for large tables where only a small portion of the table is accessed frequently. BRIN uses summary information to quickly locate data within a range of blocks. To create a BRIN index in PostgreSQL, use the following command:

CREATE INDEX idx_orders_date ON sales.orders USING BRIN (order_date);

This creates a BRIN index on the "order_date" column in the "orders" table.

Choosing Right Indexing Technique

The choice of indexing technique depends on the nature of the data and the types of queries that are run against the database. For example, if there are many range queries on a particular column, then a BRIN index might be the most suitable. If there are complex data types like geometric shapes, then a GiST or SP-GiST index would be the most suitable. For simple queries on numeric or text data types, a B-tree or hash index might be sufficient.

Indexing is an essential technique used to optimize database performance. PostgreSQL supports various indexing techniques such as B-tree, hash, GiST, SP-GiST, GIN, and BRIN, each designed to handle specific data types and queries. By using the appropriate indexing technique, database administrators can improve query performance and reduce the time required to execute complex queries. It is essential to note that choosing the right indexing technique requires a thorough understanding of the data and the types of queries that will be run against the database. Therefore, careful consideration should be taken before creating an index to avoid negatively impacting database performance.

Recipe#4: Building Concurrent Index

Concurrent indexing is a technique used to create an index on a table while allowing other database operations to continue running. In PostgreSQL, creating an index on a large table can take a long time and block other database operations, which can have a negative impact on database performance. Concurrent indexing allows for the creation of indexes on large tables without affecting the performance of other database operations.

Creating Concurrent Index in PostgreSQL

To create a concurrent index in PostgreSQL, we can use the CONCURRENTLY option with the CREATE INDEX command. Here is an example:

```
CREATE INDEX CONCURRENTLY idx_order_id ON sales.orders(order_id);
```

This command creates a concurrent index on the "order_id" column in the "orders" table in the "sales" schema.

When creating a concurrent index, PostgreSQL performs the following steps:
- PostgreSQL creates a new temporary index on the table, which takes additional disk space.
- PostgreSQL scans the table to build the index. During this process, the table is locked for write operations, but read operations are allowed.
- Once the new index is built, PostgreSQL swaps the old index with the new index. This step requires a brief table lock, during which all write operations are blocked.
- PostgreSQL drops the old index, freeing up disk space.

Advantages and Disadvantages of Concurrent Indexing

Concurrent indexing has several advantages over traditional indexing, including:

- Improved performance: Concurrent indexing allows other database operations to continue running, which can improve database performance.
- Reduced downtime: Concurrent indexing reduces the amount of downtime required to create an index on a large table.
- Flexibility: Concurrent indexing allows for the creation of indexes on large tables without affecting the performance of other database operations.

However, concurrent indexing also has some disadvantages, including:

- Increased resource requirements: Concurrent indexing requires more system resources than traditional indexing, which can slow down other database operations.
- Longer indexing times: Concurrent indexing can take longer to create than traditional indexing.
- Additional disk space: Concurrent indexing requires additional disk space to create a temporary index.
- Not suitable for all scenarios: Concurrent indexing may not be suitable for all scenarios, such as when there are heavy write operations on the table.

When to Use Concurrent Indexing?

Concurrent indexing should be used when creating an index on a large table that is frequently accessed, and when other database operations cannot be interrupted. It is especially useful when the database is being accessed by many users simultaneously, and database downtime is not an option.

It is essential to note that concurrent indexing may not be suitable for all scenarios. In particular, it may not be suitable when there are heavy write operations on the table, as creating a concurrent index requires locking the table for write operations during the indexing process.

Concurrent indexing is a useful technique that can improve database performance by allowing the creation of indexes on large tables while allowing other database operations to continue running. While concurrent indexing has several advantages, including improved performance and reduced downtime, it also has some disadvantages, including increased resource requirements and longer indexing times. Database administrators should carefully consider the specific requirements of their database and use concurrent indexing only when it is suitable for their specific scenario.

Recipe#5: Prepare Database Log Directory

The PostgreSQL database log directory is a directory used to store log files containing information about database activity and errors. The log directory is important for database administrators to monitor database activity, troubleshoot errors, and improve database performance. In this recipe, we will explain how to prepare the log directory for the AdventureWorks database.

Creating Log Directory for AdventureWorks Database

To prepare the log directory for the AdventureWorks database, follow these steps:

- Create a directory for the log files

We can create a directory for the log files using the following command:

```
sudo mkdir /var/log/postgresql
```

This creates a directory called "postgresql" in the "/var/log" directory.

- Change the ownership of the directory to the postgres user

To change the ownership of the directory to the postgres user, we can use the following command:

```
sudo chown postgres:postgres /var/log/postgresql
```

This command changes the ownership of the "postgresql" directory to the "postgres" user.

- Edit the PostgreSQL configuration file to specify the log directory

To specify the log directory in the PostgreSQL configuration file, we need to edit the "postgresql.conf" file. We can do this using the following command:

```
sudo nano /etc/postgresql/12/main/postgresql.conf
```

This command opens the PostgreSQL configuration file in the nano text editor.

Find the line that starts with 'logging_collector' and uncomment it by removing the '#'

character:
The "logging_collector" parameter is used to enable the PostgreSQL logging collector, which collects log messages and writes them to a file. We need to uncomment this parameter by removing the '#' character at the beginning of the line.

logging_collector = on

- Find the line that starts with 'log_directory' and specify the log directory

The "log_directory" parameter specifies the directory where the log files will be stored. We need to specify the directory we created earlier:

log_directory = '/var/log/postgresql'

- Save and exit the configuration file

After making the changes, we need to save the file and exit the text editor.

- Restart the PostgreSQL server to apply the changes

To apply the changes, we need to restart the PostgreSQL server using the following command:

sudo systemctl restart postgresql

This command restarts the PostgreSQL service, and the changes we made to the configuration file will take effect.

In this recipe, we have explained how to prepare the log directory for the AdventureWorks database. By following these steps, database administrators can create a directory for the log files, specify the log directory in the PostgreSQL configuration file, and restart the PostgreSQL server to apply the changes.

Recipe#6: Using PostgreSQL TOAST

PostgreSQL TOAST (The Oversized-Attribute Storage Technique) is a mechanism used to store large data types like text, XML, and binary data. It compresses the large data types and stores them in a separate table to save disk space. In this recipe, we will explain how to use TOAST in the AdventureWorks database.

Using TOAST in AdventureWorks Database

To use TOAST in the AdventureWorks database, we can follow these steps:

- Create a table with a large data type column:

We can create a table with a large data type column using the following SQL command:

```
CREATE TABLE production.product_descriptions (
  product_id INT PRIMARY KEY,
  description TEXT
);
```

In the above example, we created a table called "product_descriptions" in the "production" schema with two columns: "product_id" and "description." The "description" column is a large data type column that will be stored using TOAST.

- Insert data into the table:

We can insert data into the "product_descriptions" table using the following SQL command:

```
INSERT INTO production.product_descriptions VALUES
(1, 'Lorem ipsum dolor sit amet, consectetur adipiscing elit.'),
(2, 'Nulla facilisi. Vestibulum eleifend augue ut turpis suscipit, at varius enim sagittis.'),
(3, 'Phasellus consectetur, dolor sit amet efficitur porttitor, nunc lacus sollicitudin orci, vel lobortis arcu justo vel nibh.'),
(4, 'Donec gravida felis quis enim dapibus, vel eleifend turpis tempor.'),
(5, 'Nam porttitor elementum risus, id iaculis enim semper ut.');
```

In the above example, we inserted five rows of data into the "product_descriptions" table.

- View the TOAST table:

To see the TOAST table created for the "description" column, we can use the following SQL command:

```sql
SELECT * FROM pg_toast.pg_toast_394;
```

Note that the name of the TOAST table depends on the table and column name. In this case, the name is "pg_toast_394."

In this recipe, we explained how to use TOAST in the AdventureWorks database by creating a table with a large data type column, inserting data into the table, and viewing the TOAST table created for the "description" column. By using TOAST, database administrators can save disk space and improve database performance when working with large data types in PostgreSQL.

Recipe#7: Create and Administer PostgreSQL Temporary Table

PostgreSQL temporary tables are tables that exist only for the duration of a database session. They are used to store temporary data that is not needed beyond the current transaction or session. In this recipe, we will explain how to use temporary tables in the AdventureWorks database.

Using Temporary Tables in AdventureWorks Database

To create a temporary table in the AdventureWorks database, we can use the following SQL command:

```sql
CREATE TEMP TABLE sales.temp_orders AS SELECT * FROM sales.orders WHERE order_date = '2023-03-22';
```

In the above example, we created a temporary table named "temp_orders" in the "sales" schema. The table was created using the "orders" table as a source, and only rows where the "order_date" is '2023-03-22' were copied into the temporary table.

To drop a temporary table, we can use the following SQL command:

```sql
DROP TABLE sales.temp_orders;
```

Note that temporary tables are automatically dropped at the end of the session or transaction, so there is no need to explicitly drop them.

Temporary tables can be useful in situations where we need to store intermediate results during complex queries or data transformations. They can also be used in stored procedures to store temporary data during the execution of the procedure.

In this recipe, we explained how to use temporary tables in the AdventureWorks database by creating a temporary table based on the "orders" table and dropping it. By using temporary tables, database administrators can improve query performance and simplify data transformations in PostgreSQL.

Recipe#8: Using SELECT in WITH Queries

In PostgreSQL, WITH queries, also known as Common Table Expressions (CTE), are used to define a temporary result set that can be used in a subsequent query. The WITH clause can contain one or more SELECT statements that define the result set. In this recipe, we will explain how to use SELECT in WITH queries in the AdventureWorks database.

Using SELECT in WITH Queries

To use SELECT in WITH queries in the AdventureWorks database, we can use the following example SQL command:

```
WITH sales_today AS (
  SELECT * FROM sales.orders WHERE order_date = '2023-03-22'
)
SELECT COUNT(*) FROM sales_today;
```

In the above example, we defined a CTE named 'sales_today' that contains all orders placed on '2023-03-22'. The subsequent SELECT statement counts the number of rows in the 'sales_today' result set.

The WITH clause can also be used to define multiple CTEs, which can then be used in a subsequent query. Here is an example:

```
WITH
  sales_today AS (
```

```sql
    SELECT * FROM sales.orders WHERE order_date = '2023-03-22'
),
sales_yesterday AS (
    SELECT * FROM sales.orders WHERE order_date = '2023-03-21'
)
SELECT
  COUNT(*) as today_count,
  SUM(order_total) as today_sales,
  COUNT(*) FILTER (WHERE order_status = 'Shipped') as today_shipped,
  COUNT(*) FILTER (WHERE order_status = 'Canceled') as today_canceled,
  COUNT(*) FILTER (WHERE order_status = 'On Hold') as today_on_hold,
  (SELECT COUNT(*) FROM sales_yesterday) as yesterday_count
FROM sales_today;
```

In the above example, we defined two CTEs named 'sales_today' and 'sales_yesterday'. The subsequent SELECT statement calculates various statistics based on orders placed on '2023-03-22'. The query also includes a subquery that counts the number of orders placed on '2023-03-21' using the 'sales_yesterday' CTE.

In this recipe, we explained how to use SELECT in WITH queries in the AdventureWorks database by defining a CTE that contained all orders placed on a particular date and using the result set in a subsequent query. By using CTEs, database administrators can simplify complex queries and improve query performance in PostgreSQL.

Recipe#9: Running Recursive Query

PostgreSQL supports recursive queries using the WITH RECURSIVE clause. A recursive query is a query that refers to its own output in the query definition, and it is used to query hierarchical data like organizational charts or product categories. In this recipe, we will explain how to run a recursive query in the AdventureWorks database.

Running Recursive Query in AdventureWorks Database

To run a recursive query in the AdventureWorks database, we can use the following example:

```sql
WITH RECURSIVE product_categories AS (
  SELECT category_id, category_name, parent_category_id
  FROM production.categories
  WHERE parent_category_id IS NULL
  UNION ALL
  SELECT c.category_id, c.category_name, c.parent_category_id
  FROM production.categories c
  JOIN product_categories pc ON pc.category_id = c.parent_category_id
)
SELECT * FROM product_categories;
```

In the above example, we defined a recursive CTE (common table expression) named 'product_categories' that starts with the top-level categories that have a NULL parent_category_id. The subsequent SELECT statement selects all rows from the 'product_categories' CTE, which includes all categories and their parent-child relationships.

The recursive CTE is defined using the WITH RECURSIVE clause, which specifies the name of the CTE ('product_categories') and the initial SELECT statement that defines the base case for the recursion. The UNION ALL operator is used to combine the output of the base case with the output of the recursive case.

The recursive case is defined using another SELECT statement that joins the 'categories' table with the 'product_categories' CTE using the 'category_id' and 'parent_category_id' columns. This creates a recursive loop that traverses the hierarchy of categories until all categories have been included in the CTE.

In this recipe, we explained how to run a recursive query in the AdventureWorks database using a CTE named 'product_categories'. By using recursive queries, database administrators can simplify complex queries and improve query performance in PostgreSQL.

Recipe#10: Writing Common Table Expression (CTE)

Common Table Expressions (CTE) is a feature of PostgreSQL that allows the creation of a named temporary result set that can be used in a subsequent query. It is similar to a derived table or subquery, but it provides a more readable and reusable way to define complex queries. CTEs can reference other CTEs or tables and can be used to simplify queries that require multiple joins or subqueries.

CTE Syntax

The syntax for creating a CTE in PostgreSQL is as follows:

```
WITH cte_name (column1, column2, ...) AS (
    SELECT column1, column2, ...
    FROM table_name
    WHERE condition
)
SELECT *
FROM cte_name;
```

In this syntax, cte_name is the name given to the CTE, and column1, column2, and so on are the columns returned by the SELECT statement. The SELECT statement is used to define the temporary result set for the CTE.

Writing CTE Queries

To illustrate the usage of CTEs, let's consider an example in the AdventureWorks database. Suppose we want to retrieve the top 10 customers who have made the most purchases in the last month. We can use a CTE to accomplish this as shown below:

```
WITH customer_sales AS (
  SELECT customer_id, SUM(total_due) as total_sales
  FROM sales.orders
  WHERE order_date >= '2023-02-01' AND order_date < '2023-03-01'
  GROUP BY customer_id
  ORDER BY total_sales DESC
  LIMIT 10
)
SELECT c.customer_id, c.first_name, c.last_name, cs.total_sales
FROM customer_sales cs
```

JOIN sales.customers c ON cs.customer_id = c.customer_id;

In the above example, we created a CTE named customer_sales that sums the total sales for each customer in the last month and sorts them in descending order. The LIMIT 10 clause limits the results to the top 10 customers. The subsequent SELECT statement joins the customer_sales CTE with the sales.customers table to get the customer details.

Multiple CTEs

CTEs can also be used to simplify queries that require multiple joins or subqueries. For example, suppose we want to retrieve the products that have not been sold in the last month. We can use a CTE to accomplish this as shown below:

```
WITH last_month_orders AS (
  SELECT product_id, SUM(quantity) as total_quantity
  FROM sales.orders
  WHERE order_date >= '2023-02-01' AND order_date < '2023-03-01'
  GROUP BY product_id
),
all_products AS (
  SELECT product_id, product_name
  FROM production.products
)
SELECT ap.product_name
FROM all_products ap
LEFT JOIN last_month_orders lmo ON ap.product_id = lmo.product_id
WHERE lmo.product_id IS NULL;
```

In the above example, we created two CTEs: last_month_orders that sums the quantity of each product sold in the last month and all_products that retrieves all products. The subsequent SELECT statement joins the all_products CTE with the last_month_orders CTE using a left join to get all products that have not been sold in the last month.

In summary, Common Table Expressions (CTE) is a powerful feature of PostgreSQL that allows the creation of a temporary result set that can be used in a subsequent query. CTEs can simplify queries that require multiple joins or subqueries and can improve query readability.

Chapter 3: PostgreSQL Cloud Provisioning

Recipe#1: Create PostgreSQL Cloud Instance and Manage Database Connection with AWS EC2 and RDS

Creating a PostgreSQL Cloud Instance and Managing Database Connection with AWS EC2 for the AdventureWorks Database:

Setup AWS Account

To begin, sign up for an Amazon Web Services (AWS) account if you haven't already: https://aws.amazon.com/

Once you have an account, log in to the AWS Management Console and choose your desired region from the top-right corner.

Create Amazon RDS PostgreSQL Instance

In the AWS Management Console, search for "RDS" and click on "RDS – Managed Relational Database Service".

In the RDS Dashboard, click on "Create database" and choose "Standard Create" as the creation method.

Select "PostgreSQL" as the engine type and choose the desired version.

In the "Templates" section, select "Free tier" for experimentation or choose "Production" for a more robust setup.

In the "Settings" section, provide a unique DB instance identifier, master username, and password. Save these credentials for future reference.

In the "DB instance size" section, choose the appropriate instance class based on your needs.

Expand the "Storage" section and configure the storage type, allocated storage, and storage autoscaling as needed.

In the "Connectivity" section, choose the appropriate VPC, subnet group, and enable "Publicly accessible" if you want to access the database from outside the VPC.

Set up a new security group or choose an existing one to manage access to the instance. Make a note of the security group, as it will be needed later.

In the "Database authentication" section, select "Password authentication".

Expand the "Additional configuration" section and set the initial database name to "adventureworks".

Configure backups, monitoring, and maintenance options as desired.

Click on "Create database" to begin the provisioning process. It may take a few minutes to complete.

Download and Extract AdventureWorks Database

Download the AdventureWorks PostgreSQL database sample from the provided link: https://github.com/kittenpub/database-repository/blob/main/data.zip

Extract the contents of the "data.zip" file to a folder on your local machine.

Modify Security Group to Allow Inbound Traffic

In the AWS Management Console, search for "EC2" and click on "EC2 – Virtual Servers in the Cloud".

In the EC2 Dashboard, click on "Security Groups" under "Network & Security" in the left-hand menu.

Find the security group associated with your RDS instance and click on the "Inbound rules" tab.

Click on "Edit inbound rules" and add a new rule with the following settings:

Type: PostgreSQL
Protocol: TCP
Port range: 5432
Source: Custom (enter your IP address or the IP address range of the systems that need access)

Click on "Save rules" to apply the changes.

Connect to RDS Instance and Import AdventureWorks Database

Install pgAdmin, a popular PostgreSQL management tool, on your local machine: https://www.pgadmin.org/download/

Open pgAdmin and click on "Add New Server" to create a new connection.

In the "General" tab, provide a name for the connection.

In the "Connection" tab, enter the endpoint of your RDS instance (available in the RDS Dashboard) as the "Hostname/Address" and use port "5432". Enter the master username and password you set up earlier.

Click "Save" to create the connection. You should now see your RDS instance in the list of servers on the left side of pgAdmin.

Connect to the "adventureworks" database and right-click on it, then select "Query Tool" to open a new query editor.

Open the extracted AdventureWorks SQL file from the "data.zip" archive in a text editor. Copy the entire content and paste it into the query editor in pgAdmin.

Click on the "Execute" button (or press the F5 key) to run the SQL commands. This process will create tables and import data into the "adventureworks" database. It may take some time to complete.

Launch EC2 Instance

In the AWS Management Console, search for "EC2" and click on "EC2 – Virtual Servers in the Cloud".

Click on "Instances" in the left-hand menu and then click the "Launch Instance" button.

Choose an Amazon Machine Image (AMI) that meets your requirements. For example, you can use the "Amazon Linux 2 AMI" for a Linux-based instance.

Choose an instance type based on your performance and budget requirements, then click "Next: Configure Instance Details".
Configure the instance details as needed, making sure to select the same VPC as your RDS

instance. Click "Next: Add Storage".

Configure storage as needed and click "Next: Add Tags".

Add any desired tags for identification and click "Next: Configure Security Group".

Create a new security group or select an existing one. Confirm to add rules to allow traffic for your desired services (e.g., SSH, HTTP, or HTTPS). Click "Review and Launch".

Review your instance settings and click "Launch".

A dialog box will prompt you to select or create a key pair. Choose an existing key pair or create a new one, then download the private key file (.pem) and store it in a secure location.

Click "Launch Instances" to start the provisioning process.

Configure EC2 Instance and Connect to RDS PostgreSQL Instance

SSH into your EC2 instance using the private key file (.pem) and the appropriate user (e.g., "ec2-user" for Amazon Linux 2).

Update the package repositories and install the PostgreSQL client:

```
sudo yum update -y
sudo yum install -y postgresql
```

Use the "psql" command to connect to the RDS PostgreSQL instance:

```
psql --host=<RDS_ENDPOINT> --port=5432 --username=<MASTER_USERNAME> --password --dbname=adventureworks
```

Replace <RDS_ENDPOINT> with the endpoint of your RDS instance, and <MASTER_USERNAME> with the master username you set up earlier.

You should now be connected to the "adventureworks" database on your RDS instance. You can execute SQL queries and manage the database as needed.

By following these steps, you have successfully created a PostgreSQL cloud instance on

AWS RDS and connected it to an EC2 instance. You have also imported the AdventureWorks sample database, allowing you to manage and interact with it using pgAdmin and the PostgreSQL client on the EC2 instance.

Recipe#2: Native Backup/Restore with AWS EC2 Instance

Create Backup Directory on EC2 Instance

SSH into your EC2 instance using the private key file (.pem) and the appropriate user (e.g., "ec2-user" for Amazon Linux 2).

Create a backup directory on your EC2 instance to store the database backup files:

```
mkdir ~/adventureworks_backups
```

Backup AdventureWorks Database using pg_dump

Install the PostgreSQL client on the EC2 instance if you haven't already:

```
sudo yum update -y
sudo yum install -y postgresql
```

Use the pg_dump command to create a backup of the AdventureWorks database:

```
pg_dump --host=<RDS_ENDPOINT> --port=5432 --
username=<MASTER_USERNAME> --password --format=custom --
file=~/adventureworks_backups/adventureworks_backup.dump --
dbname=adventureworks
```

Replace <RDS_ENDPOINT> with the endpoint of your RDS instance, and <MASTER_USERNAME> with the master username you set up earlier.
Enter your master password when prompted. The backup process will create a binary dump file named "adventureworks_backup.dump" in the "adventureworks_backups" directory.

Transfer Backup File to Amazon S3 for Long-term Storage

Install the AWS CLI on your EC2 instance:

```
sudo yum install -y awscli
```

Configure the AWS CLI by running:

```
aws configure
```

Enter your AWS Access Key, Secret Access Key, default region, and output format when prompted.

Create a new Amazon S3 bucket to store the backup files:

```
aws s3api create-bucket --bucket adventureworks-backups-<YOUR_NAME> --region <YOUR_REGION> --create-bucket-configuration LocationConstraint=<YOUR_REGION>
```

Replace <YOUR_NAME> with a unique identifier, and <YOUR_REGION> with the region in which you want to create the bucket.

Upload the backup file to the Amazon S3 bucket:

```
aws s3 cp ~/adventureworks_backups/adventureworks_backup.dump s3://adventureworks-backups-<YOUR_NAME>/adventureworks_backup.dump
```

Replace <YOUR_NAME> with the unique identifier you used when creating the bucket.

Restore Database from Backup File Using pg_restore

To restore the database, you first need to create a new empty database on the RDS instance. Connect to the RDS instance using the "psql" command:

```
psql --host=<RDS_ENDPOINT> --port=5432 --username=<MASTER_USERNAME> --password --dbname=postgres
```

Replace <RDS_ENDPOINT> with the endpoint of your RDS instance, and <MASTER_USERNAME> with the master username you set up earlier.

Enter your master password when prompted, and run the following SQL command to create a new empty database named "adventureworks_restore":

CREATE DATABASE adventureworks_restore;

Exit the "psql" command-line interface by typing \q and pressing Enter.

Use the "pg_restore" command to restore the AdventureWorks database from the backup file to the newly created "adventureworks_restore" database:

```
pg_restore --host=<RDS_ENDPOINT> --port=5432 --
username=<MASTER_USERNAME> --password --
dbname=adventureworks_restore --verbose
~/adventureworks_backups/adventureworks_backup
pg_restore --host=<RDS_ENDPOINT> --port=5432 --
username=<MASTER_USERNAME> --password --
dbname=adventureworks_restore --verbose
~/adventureworks_backups/adventureworks_backup.dump
```

Replace <RDS_ENDPOINT> with the endpoint of your RDS instance, and <MASTER_USERNAME> with the master username you set up earlier.

Enter your master password when prompted. The restore process will begin, and you will see a verbose output of the restoration progress. Once completed, the "adventureworks_restore" database should contain the same data as the original "adventureworks" database.

Verify Restoration

Connect to the "adventureworks_restore" database using the "psql" command:

```
psql --host=<RDS_ENDPOINT> --port=5432 --
username=<MASTER_USERNAME> --password --
```

dbname=adventureworks_restore

Replace <RDS_ENDPOINT> with the endpoint of your RDS instance, and <MASTER_USERNAME> with the master username you set up earlier.

Enter your master password when prompted, and run the following SQL command to verify that the restored database contains the same tables as the original database:

```
\dt
```

You should see a list of tables that match the original "adventureworks" database.

You can also run SELECT queries on the restored database to ensure the data is intact and matches the original database.

By following these steps, you have successfully backed up and restored the AdventureWorks database using native PostgreSQL tools on an AWS EC2 instance. You have also learned how to store the backup files on Amazon S3 for long-term storage and transfer the backup files between your EC2 instance and Amazon S3.

Recipe#3: Natively Backup/Restore with AWS RDS Instance

In AWS RDS, backups can be managed automatically with snapshots, or you can create manual snapshots. This recipe will cover both methods and demonstrate how to restore the database from a snapshot.

Enable Automated Backups for RDS Instance

In the AWS Management Console, navigate to the RDS Dashboard.

Click on "Databases" in the left-hand menu and select the RDS instance hosting the AdventureWorks database.

In the "Details" tab, click on the "Modify" button.

Scroll down to the "Backup" section and set the "Backup retention period" to a value greater than 0 (e.g., 7 days). This will enable automated backups.

Choose the preferred backup window or let AWS choose it for you by selecting "No preference."

Click on "Continue" and choose whether to apply the changes immediately or during the next maintenance window. Then, click on "Modify DB Instance."

Create Manual Snapshot of Database

In the RDS Dashboard, click on "Databases" in the left-hand menu and select the RDS instance hosting the AdventureWorks database.

In the "Details" tab, click on the "Actions" button and choose "Take snapshot."

Provide a unique name for the snapshot and click on the "Take snapshot" button. The snapshot creation process will begin and may take some time to complete.

Restore Database from Snapshot

In the RDS Dashboard, click on "Snapshots" in the left-hand menu.

Select the snapshot you want to restore from (either an automated backup or a manual snapshot).

Click on the "Actions" button and choose "Restore snapshot."

In the "Restore DB Instance" page, provide a unique name for the new RDS instance that will be created from the snapshot.

Configure the DB instance settings, such as instance class, storage type, and storage size, as needed.

In the "Settings" section, provide a new master username and password for the restored instance.

Choose the appropriate VPC, subnet group, and security group for the restored instance. Ensure that the security group allows inbound traffic for PostgreSQL on port 5432.

Configure any additional settings as needed, such as "Database authentication," "Backup," "Monitoring," and "Maintenance."

Click on "Restore DB Instance" to begin the restoration process. It may take some time to complete.

Verify Restored Database

Once the restored RDS instance is available, connect to it using a PostgreSQL client, such as pgAdmin or psql, with the new master username and password.

In the client, connect to the "adventureworks" database and verify the tables and data by running SQL queries. The restored database should contain the same data as the original database at the time of the snapshot.

Point Your Application to Restored Database

If you want to use the restored database instead of the original one, update your application's database connection settings to point to the endpoint of the restored RDS instance. Confirm to update any necessary credentials as well.

By following these steps, you have successfully backed up and restored the AdventureWorks database using native AWS RDS features, such as automated backups and manual snapshots. These methods provide a simple and efficient way to manage database backups in the AWS cloud without needing to use traditional PostgreSQL tools like pg_dump and pg_restore.

Recipe#4: Manage Connection to Database on AWS

Configure Security Groups

Ensuring the security of your database connection is crucial. You can start by configuring the security group associated with your RDS instance to allow incoming connections from specific IP addresses or ranges. Following are the steps:

- In the AWS Management Console, navigate to the RDS Dashboard.

- Click on "Databases" in the left-hand menu and select the RDS instance hosting the AdventureWorks database.

- In the "Details" tab, locate the "Security group rules" section, click on the security group.

- In the "Inbound rules" tab, click on the "Edit inbound rules" button.

- Add a new rule with the following settings:

Type: PostgreSQL
Protocol: TCP
Port range: 5432

- In Source, Choose "Custom" and enter the IP address or range you want to allow, or use "My IP" to allow only your current IP address.

- Click on "Save rules" to apply the changes.

Use Connection Pooler

Connection pooling helps improve performance and manage database connections efficiently by reusing existing connections instead of opening and closing new connections for each request.

One popular connection pooler for PostgreSQL is PgBouncer. To install and configure PgBouncer on an EC2 instance, follow these steps:

SSH into your EC2 instance using the private key file (.pem) and the appropriate user (e.g., "ec2-user" for Amazon Linux 2).

Update the package repositories and install PgBouncer:

```
sudo yum update -y
sudo yum install -y pgbouncer
```

Create a directory for the PgBouncer configuration files and logs:

```
mkdir ~/pgbouncer
```

Create a new PgBouncer configuration file (pgbouncer.ini) in the newly created directory with the following content:

```
[databases]
```

adventureworks = host=<RDS_ENDPOINT> port=5432
dbname=adventureworks

[pgbouncer]
listen_addr = *
listen_port = 6432
auth_type = md5
auth_file = users.txt
logfile = pgbouncer.log
pidfile = pgbouncer.pid
admin_users = <MASTER_USERNAME>

Replace <RDS_ENDPOINT> with the endpoint of your RDS instance, and <MASTER_USERNAME> with the master username you set up earlier.

Create a new file (users.txt) in the same directory to store the authentication credentials for your RDS instance. Add the following line to the file:

"<MASTER_USERNAME>" "<MASTER_PASSWORD>"

Replace <MASTER_USERNAME> and <MASTER_PASSWORD> with the master username and password you set up earlier.

Start PgBouncer by running the following command:

pgbouncer ~/pgbouncer/pgbouncer.ini

Configure your application to connect to the PgBouncer instance by updating the connection string to use the EC2 instance's IP address or DNS name and port 6432.

Monitor Connection Metrics

Monitoring your database connections can provide valuable insights into performance, bottlenecks, and potential issues. AWS RDS offers various monitoring options, including Amazon RDS Performance Insights and Amazon CloudWatch.

Enable Amazon RDS Performance Insights

In the RDS Dashboard, click on "Databases" in the left-hand menu and select the RDS instance hosting the AdventureWorks database.

In the "Details" tab, click on the "Modify" button.

Scroll down to the "Monitoring" section and enable "Performance Insights."

Choose the desired retention period for the performance data and click on "Continue."

Choose whether to apply the changes immediately or during the next maintenance window.

Then, click on "Modify DB Instance."

Access Amazon RDS Performance Insights

In the RDS Dashboard, click on "Databases" in the left-hand menu and select the RDS instance hosting the AdventureWorks database.

In the "Details" tab, click on the "Performance Insights" link to access the Performance Insights dashboard.

Use the dashboard to analyze various metrics related to database connections, such as active connections, wait events, and query performance.

Monitor Amazon CloudWatch Metrics:

In the RDS Dashboard, click on "Databases" in the left-hand menu and select the RDS instance hosting the AdventureWorks database.

In the "Details" tab, click on the "Monitoring" tab to view the CloudWatch metrics.

Focus on the "DatabaseConnections" metric to monitor the number of connections to your RDS instance.

Optimize Application Connection Management

Implement best practices for managing connections in your application to minimize the overhead and improve performance.

Use connection strings with appropriate timeouts and limits to avoid excessive idle connections or long-running queries.

Optimize your application's connection management by closing connections when they are no longer needed.

Use a connection pooler, like PgBouncer, to efficiently manage database connections and reuse them whenever possible.

Monitor and fine-tune connection pooler settings, such as connection limits and timeouts, to optimize performance.

In summary, managing connections to the AdventureWorks PostgreSQL database on AWS involves configuring security groups, using connection poolers like PgBouncer, monitoring connection metrics with Amazon RDS Performance Insights and Amazon CloudWatch, and optimizing application connection management. Implementing these best practices will help you maintain a secure, efficient, and high-performance connection to your PostgreSQL database hosted on AWS RDS.

Recipe#5: Perform Replication of Database on AWS

To replicate the AdventureWorks PostgreSQL database on AWS, you can use Amazon RDS's built-in support for read replicas. Read replicas allow you to offload read traffic from your primary database instance, which can help balance the load and improve performance.

Enable Automatic Backups for RDS Instance

In the AWS Management Console, navigate to the RDS Dashboard.

Click on "Databases" in the left-hand menu and select the RDS instance hosting the AdventureWorks database.

In the "Details" tab, click on the "Modify" button.

Scroll down to the "Backup" section and set the "Backup retention period" to a value greater than 0 (e.g., 7 days). This will enable automatic backups, which are required for creating read replicas.

Choose the preferred backup window or let AWS choose it for you by selecting "No preference."

Click on "Continue" and choose whether to apply the changes immediately or during the next maintenance window. Then, click on "Modify DB Instance."

Create Read Replica

In the RDS Dashboard, click on "Databases" in the left-hand menu and select the RDS instance hosting the AdventureWorks database.

In the "Details" tab, click on the "Actions" button and choose "Create read replica."

Provide a unique name for the read replica instance.

Configure the DB instance settings, such as instance class, storage type, and storage size, as needed.

Choose the appropriate VPC, subnet group, and security group for the read replica instance. Ensure that the security group allows inbound traffic for PostgreSQL on port 5432.

Configure any additional settings as needed, such as "Multi-AZ deployment," "Database authentication," "Backup," "Monitoring," and "Maintenance."

Click on "Create read replica" to start the replication process. It may take some time to complete.

Verify Read Replica

Once the read replica instance is available, connect to it using a PostgreSQL client, such as pgAdmin or psql, with the master username and password.

In the client, connect to the "adventureworks" database and verify the tables and data by running SQL queries. The read replica should contain the same data as the primary database at the time of the snapshot.

Redirect Read Traffic to Read Replica

Update your application's database connection settings to direct read traffic to the read replica endpoint instead of the primary RDS instance. Depending on your application architecture, you can implement a load balancer or use custom code to distribute the read traffic among the primary and replica instances.

Monitor Replication Performance

In the RDS Dashboard, click on "Databases" in the left-hand menu and select the read replica instance.

In the "Details" tab, click on the "Monitoring" tab to view the Amazon CloudWatch metrics.

Focus on the "ReplicaLag" metric to monitor the replication lag between the primary and replica instances. Ideally, the lag should be minimal to ensure data consistency and up-to-date results for read queries.

Promote Read Replica (Optional)

If needed, you can promote a read replica to a standalone RDS instance. This is useful in disaster recovery scenarios or when you want to create a separate environment for testing or development.

In the RDS Dashboard, click on "Databases" in the left-hand menu and select the read replica instance.

In the "Details" tab, click on the "Actions"

In the "Details" tab, click on the "Actions" button and choose "Promote read replica." A warning message will appear, stating that promoting the read replica will cause it to function as a standalone instance and break the replication. Click on "Promote read replica" to proceed.

The promotion process may take some time to complete. Once it is finished, the instance will function as a standalone RDS instance, and you can manage it like any other RDS instance.

Delete Read Replica (Optional)

If you no longer need the read replica, you can delete it to save costs and resources.

In the RDS Dashboard, click on "Databases" in the left-hand menu and select the read replica instance.

In the "Details" tab, click on the "Actions" button and choose "Delete."

In the "Delete DB instance" dialog, choose whether to create a final snapshot before deleting the instance. If you want to save the current state of the database, select "Create final snapshot" and provide a unique name for the snapshot.

Check the acknowledgment box, stating that you understand that deleting the instance will result in data loss, and click on "Delete DB Instance."

By following these steps, you have practically replicated the AdventureWorks database on AWS using Amazon RDS read replicas. Read replicas help distribute the read traffic, improve performance, and provide a scalable solution for high-availability scenarios. Additionally, you can monitor replication performance using Amazon CloudWatch and manage the replica instances as needed by promoting or deleting them.

Recipe#6: Run PostgreSQL Bi-directional Replication using pglogical

Bi-directional replication, also known as multi-master replication, allows two or more PostgreSQL databases to replicate data changes between them. It is useful for load balancing and ensuring high availability in distributed environments. One of the tools available for bi-directional replication in PostgreSQL is pglogical, a logical replication extension.

In this recipe, we will assume you have two RDS instances running the AdventureWorks database, named adventureworks_primary and adventureworks_secondary. We will set up bi-directional replication between these instances using pglogical.

Enable pglogical Extension on both RDS Instances

Modify the shared_preload_libraries parameter on both instances to include pglogical. In the RDS Dashboard, select the instances and click "Modify". Under "Database options", add pglogical to the list of shared libraries.

In the same modification window, enable the rds.logical_replication parameter by setting it to 1.

Apply the changes immediately or during the next maintenance window and wait for the instances to be modified.

Connect to both RDS Instances

Use a PostgreSQL client, such as pgAdmin or psql, to connect to both RDS instances with the master username and password.

Install pglogical Extension on both Instances

On both instances, connect to the AdventureWorks database and run the following SQL command to create the pglogical extension:

```
CREATE EXTENSION pglogical;
```

Configure Replication Nodes

On both instances, create a replication node with a unique node name and connection information:

```
SELECT pglogical.create_node(
    node_name := 'adventureworks_primary_node',
    dsn := 'host=adventureworks_primary_endpoint port=5432
dbname=adventureworks user=<MASTER_USERNAME>
password=<MASTER_PASSWORD>'
);


SELECT pglogical.create_node(
    node_name := 'adventureworks_secondary_node',
    dsn := 'host=adventureworks_secondary_endpoint port=5432
dbname=adventureworks user=<MASTER_USERNAME>
password=<MASTER_PASSWORD>'
);
```

Replace the placeholders with the actual endpoint URLs, master username, and master password for your instances.

On both instances, add all tables in the AdventureWorks database to the replication set:

SELECT pglogical.replication_set_add_all_tables('default', ARRAY['public']);

On both instances, add all sequences in the AdventureWorks database to the replication set:

SELECT pglogical.replication_set_add_all_sequences('default',
ARRAY['public']);

Create Replication Subscriptions

On the primary instance, create a subscription to the secondary instance:

```
SELECT pglogical.create_subscription(
    subscription_name := 'adventureworks_primary_to_secondary',
    provider_dsn := 'host=adventureworks_secondary_endpoint port=5432
dbname=adventureworks user=<MASTER_USERNAME>
password=<MASTER_PASSWORD>',
    replication_sets := ARRAY['default'],
    synchronize_structure := false,
    synchronize_data := true
);
```

On the secondary instance, create a subscription to the primary instance:

```
SELECT pglogical.create_subscription(
    subscription_name := 'adventureworks_secondary_to_primary',
    provider_dsn := 'host=adventureworks_primary_endpoint port=5432
dbname=adventureworks user=<MASTER_USERNAME>
password=<MASTER_PASSWORD>',
    replication_sets := ARRAY['default'],
    synchronize_structure := false,
    synchronize_data := true
);
```

Replace the placeholders with the actual endpoint URLs, master username, and master password for your instances.

Verify Replication

On both instances, insert, update, or delete some data in the AdventureWorks database and verify that the changes are replicated to the other instance.

On both instances, monitor the replication status by querying the pglogical.show_subscription_status() function:

```
SELECT * FROM pglogical.show_subscription_status();
```

If the replication is working correctly, you should see the status column as 'replicating' for both subscriptions.

Troubleshooting

If you encounter any issues or replication lag, you can check the PostgreSQL logs on both instances for errors or warnings related to pglogical.

In the RDS Dashboard, click on "Databases" in the left-hand menu and select the RDS instance.

In the "Details" tab, click on the "Logs & events" tab to view the logs.

Look for any errors or warnings related to pglogical and resolve them accordingly.

Manage Replication

As your application evolves, you may need to add or remove tables, sequences, or indexes from the replication set. Use the following pglogical functions to manage the replication set:

To add a table to the replication set:

```
SELECT pglogical.replication_set_add_table('default',
'<SCHEMA_NAME>.<TABLE_NAME>');
```

To remove a table from the replication set:

```
SELECT pglogical.replication_set_remove_table('default',
'<SCHEMA_NAME>.<TABLE_NAME>');
```

To add a sequence to the replication set:

```
SELECT pglogical.replication_set_add_sequence('default',
'<SCHEMA_NAME>.<SEQUENCE_NAME>');
```

To remove a sequence from the replication set:

```
SELECT pglogical.replication_set_remove_sequence('default',
'<SCHEMA_NAME>.<SEQUENCE_NAME>');
```

By following these steps, you have practically set up bi-directional replication for the AdventureWorks database on AWS using pglogical. This replication allows you to distribute database load, improve performance, and ensure high availability in your distributed PostgreSQL environment. Additionally, you can monitor the replication status and manage the replication set using pglogical functions.

Chapter 4: Database Migration to Cloud and PostgreSQL

Recipe#1: Migrating from On-premise to AWS EC2/RDS Instance

This recipe assumes you have an on-premise PostgreSQL server hosting the AdventureWorks database and want to migrate it to an AWS EC2 or RDS instance.

Prepare On-premise Environment

Make sure your on-premise PostgreSQL server is running and accessible.

Ensure you have the necessary credentials for the PostgreSQL server (username and password).

Create Backup of AdventureWorks Database

Create a backup of the AdventureWorks database on your on-premise server using the pg_dump tool:

```
pg_dump -U <USERNAME> -W -F t -f adventureworks_backup.tar
adventureworks
```

Replace <USERNAME> with your PostgreSQL username. You will be prompted for the password.

Setup AWS Environment

If you haven't already, create an AWS account and sign in to the AWS Management Console.

Create an EC2 instance or RDS instance for hosting the AdventureWorks database, as described in previous responses.

If using RDS, ensure that the necessary extensions (e.g., postgis) are installed on the RDS instance.

Transfer Backup to AWS Environment

You need to transfer the adventureworks_backup.tar file created in Step 2 to the AWS environment. There are several methods to do this, including:

- Using SCP (for EC2 instances):

```
scp -i <PATH_TO_YOUR_PRIVATE_KEY> adventureworks_backup.tar ec2-user@<EC2_PUBLIC_DNS>:/home/ec2-user/
```

Replace <PATH_TO_YOUR_PRIVATE_KEY> with the path to your EC2 private key and <EC2_PUBLIC_DNS> with the public DNS of your EC2 instance.

- Using S3 (for RDS instances or EC2 instances):

Create an Amazon S3 bucket in the same region as your RDS/EC2 instance.

Upload the adventureworks_backup.tar file to the S3 bucket.

If using an EC2 instance, download the file from the S3 bucket to your EC2 instance.

Restore AdventureWorks Database

- If using an EC2 instance:

Install PostgreSQL on the EC2 instance, if not already installed.

- Create an empty AdventureWorks database:

```
createdb -U <USERNAME> -W adventureworks
```

- Restore the backup to the new database:

```
pg_restore -U <USERNAME> -W -d adventureworks adventureworks_backup.tar
```

- If using an RDS instance:

Create an empty AdventureWorks database using a PostgreSQL client, such as pgAdmin or psql:
sql

```
CREATE DATABASE adventureworks;
```

- Restore the backup to the new database using the pg_restore tool, connecting to the RDS instance:

```
pg_restore -h <RDS_ENDPOINT> -U <MASTER_USERNAME> -W -d
adventureworks adventureworks_backup.tar
```

Replace <RDS_ENDPOINT> and <MASTER_USERNAME> with your RDS instance's endpoint and master username, respectively.

Update Application Settings

Update your application's database connection settings to point to the new AWS EC2 or RDS instance.

Verify Migration

Connect to the AdventureWorks database on the AWS EC2 or RDS instance using a PostgreSQL client, such as pgAdmin or psql.

Run some SQL queries to verify the tables, data, and other objects have been migrated correctly.

Monitor and Optimize

Monitor the performance and resource usage of your EC2 or RDS instance and optimize as needed. You can use Amazon CloudWatch to monitor AWS resources and set up alerts for specific events.

For EC2 instances, you can monitor CPU utilization, disk I/O, and network traffic, among other metrics.

For RDS instances, you can monitor additional database-specific metrics such as the number of database connections, read and write IOPS, and query latency.

Depending on your findings, you may need to:
- Scale the EC2 or RDS instance vertically by increasing the instance size (CPU, memory, and storage).
- Optimize the PostgreSQL configuration parameters for better performance, such as shared_buffers, effective_cache_size, and maintenance_work_mem.
- Analyze and optimize slow-running queries using the EXPLAIN command or

other query profiling tools.
- Implement caching, indexing, and partitioning strategies to improve database performance.

By following these steps, you have practically migrated the AdventureWorks database from an on-premise PostgreSQL server to an AWS EC2 or RDS instance. Migration to AWS provides benefits such as scalability, high availability, and the ability to leverage various AWS services for monitoring and optimization.

Recipe#2: Utilizing AWS Data Migration Service (DMS)

AWS Data Migration Service (DMS) simplifies migrating your databases to the AWS Cloud, while minimizing downtime. DMS can migrate your data to and from most widely used commercial and open-source databases, including PostgreSQL.

In this recipe, we'll walk through the process of migrating the AdventureWorks database from an on-premise PostgreSQL server to an Amazon RDS for PostgreSQL instance using AWS DMS.

Prepare On-premise Environment

Make sure your on-premise PostgreSQL server is running and accessible. Ensure you have the necessary credentials for the PostgreSQL server (username and password).

Setup AWS Environment

If you haven't already, create an AWS account and sign in to the AWS Management Console.

Create an Amazon RDS for PostgreSQL instance, as described in previous responses, to host the AdventureWorks database.

Create VPC Peering Connection (Optional)

If your on-premise PostgreSQL server is hosted in an Amazon VPC, you may need to create a VPC peering connection between the VPC hosting your on-premise server and the VPC hosting the RDS instance.

In the AWS Management Console, navigate to the VPC Dashboard.

Click on "Peering Connections" in the left-hand menu and click on the "Create Peering Connection" button.

Provide the VPC IDs for both the requester and accepter VPCs and click "Create Peering Connection".

Accept the peering connection request on the accepter VPC side.

Create AWS DMS Replication Instance

In the AWS Management Console, navigate to the DMS Dashboard.

Click on "Replication instances" in the left-hand menu and click on the "Create replication instance" button.

Provide a name and description for the replication instance, choose an instance class, and set the allocated storage.

Select the VPC that contains your on-premise PostgreSQL server and RDS instance (or the VPCs connected by the peering connection), then click "Create" to launch the replication instance.

Create Source and Target Endpoints

In the DMS Dashboard, click on "Endpoints" in the left-hand menu and click on the "Create endpoint" button.

Create a source endpoint for your on-premise PostgreSQL server:

Select "Source endpoint".

Provide an endpoint identifier, source engine (PostgreSQL), and connection information for your on-premise PostgreSQL server, including server name, port, username, and password.
Click "Create endpoint".

Create a target endpoint for your RDS instance:

Select "Target endpoint".

Provide an endpoint identifier, target engine (PostgreSQL), and connection information for your RDS instance, including server name, port, username, and password.

Click "Create endpoint".

Test Endpoints

In the "Endpoints" section of the DMS Dashboard, select the source endpoint and click on the "Test connection" button.

Choose the replication instance you created earlier and click "Run test".

The test should return a "successful" status. If not, troubleshoot the connection issues.

Repeat the test for the target endpoint.

Create Database Migration Task

In the DMS Dashboard, click on "Database migration tasks" in the left-hand menu and click on the "Create task" button.

Provide a name and description for the migration task.

Select the replication instance, source endpoint, and target endpoint you created earlier.

Choose a migration type. For a one-time migration, choose "Migrate existing data" (Full Load).

If you want to replicate ongoing changes after the full load, choose "Migrate existing data and replicate ongoing changes" (Full Load + CDC).

Under "Task Settings", configure any additional settings you need, such as:

Enable logging: If you want to log detailed information about the migration process.

Stop task after full load completes: If you want the task to stop automatically after the full load phase.

Target table preparation mode: You can choose "Do nothing", "Drop tables on target", or "Truncate" depending on how you want the target tables to be prepared before the migration.

Under "Table mappings", create rules to specify which tables and schemas to migrate. For the AdventureWorks database, you can create a single rule with the source schema set to "public" and the target schema set to "public". Ensure the selection rule action is set to "Include".

Click "Create task" to create the migration task.

Start the Migration Task

In the "Database migration tasks" section of the DMS Dashboard, select the migration task you created.

Click on the "Start/Resume" button to start the migration process.

Monitor the progress of the migration task. You can view the status, progress, and any warnings or errors in the DMS Dashboard.

Verify the Migration

Connect to the AdventureWorks database on the RDS instance using a PostgreSQL client, such as pgAdmin or psql.

Run some SQL queries to verify the tables, data, and other objects have been migrated correctly.

Monitor and Optimize

Monitor the performance and resource usage of your RDS instance and DMS replication instance, and optimize as needed. You can use Amazon CloudWatch to monitor AWS resources and set up alerts for specific events.

Depending on your findings, you may need to:

Scale the RDS instance vertically by increasing the instance size (CPU, memory, and storage).

Optimize the PostgreSQL configuration parameters for better performance, such as shared_buffers, effective_cache_size, and maintenance_work_mem.

Analyze and optimize slow-running queries using the EXPLAIN command or other query profiling tools.

Implement caching, indexing, and partitioning strategies to improve database performance.

By following these steps, you have practically migrated the AdventureWorks database from an on-premise PostgreSQL server to an Amazon RDS for PostgreSQL instance using AWS Data Migration Service. DMS simplifies the migration process and minimizes downtime, allowing you to benefit from the scalability, high availability, and various AWS services for monitoring and optimization.

Recipe#3: Migrating Database from EC2 to RDS Instance

This recipe assumes you have the AdventureWorks database hosted on an Amazon EC2 instance and want to migrate it to an Amazon RDS instance.

Prepare EC2 Environment

Make sure your EC2 instance hosting the PostgreSQL server is running and accessible. Ensure you have the necessary credentials for the PostgreSQL server (username and password).

Create Backup of AdventureWorks Database

Create a backup of the AdventureWorks database on your EC2 instance using the pg_dump tool:

```
pg_dump -U <USERNAME> -W -F t -f adventureworks_backup.tar
adventureworks
```

Replace <USERNAME> with your PostgreSQL username. You will be prompted for the password.

Setup RDS Environment

If you haven't already, create an AWS account and sign in to the AWS Management Console.

Create an Amazon RDS for PostgreSQL instance to host the AdventureWorks database, as described in previous responses.

Transfer Backup to RDS Environment

Upload the adventureworks_backup.tar file created in Step 2 to an Amazon S3 bucket:

Create an Amazon S3 bucket in the same region as your RDS instance.

Upload the adventureworks_backup.tar file to the S3 bucket.

Grant RDS Access to S3 Bucket

Create an IAM role that grants your RDS instance permission to access the S3 bucket:

In the AWS Management Console, navigate to the IAM Dashboard.

Click on "Roles" in the left-hand menu and click on the "Create role" button.

Select "RDS" as the service that will use this role and click "Next: Permissions".

Search for "AmazonS3ReadOnlyAccess" in the "Filter policies" search box, select the policy, and click "Next: Tags".

Add any tags you need and click "Next: Review".

Provide a name and description for the role and click "Create role".

In the RDS Dashboard, click on "Databases" in the left-hand menu and select the RDS instance.

In the "Details" tab, click on the "Modify" button.

In the "Database options" section, set the "IAM DB authentication" option to "Enabled" and select the IAM role you just created for the "S3 import/export role" option.

Click "Continue" and choose "Apply immediately" in the confirmation dialog.

Restore AdventureWorks Database

Create an empty AdventureWorks database on your RDS instance using a PostgreSQL client, such as pgAdmin or psql:

CREATE DATABASE adventureworks;

Use the AWS CLI to execute the aws rds restore-db-instance-from-s3 command to restore the backup from the S3 bucket to the AdventureWorks database on the RDS instance:

```
aws rds restore-db-instance-from-s3 \
  --db-instance-identifier <RDS_INSTANCE_IDENTIFIER> \
  --db-instance-class <RDS_INSTANCE_CLASS> \
  --engine postgres \
  --master-username <MASTER_USERNAME> \
  --master-user-password <MASTER_USER_PASSWORD> \
  --vpc-security-group-ids <VPC_SECURITY_GROUP_ID> \
  --s3-bucket-name <BUCKET_NAME> \
  --s3-prefix adventureworks_backup.tar \
  --source-engine postgres \
  --source-engine-version <SOURCE_ENGINE_VERSION> \
  --region <AWS_REGION> \
  --availability-zone <AVAILABILITY
_ZONE>
--no-multi-az
--no-publicly-accessible
--db-name adventureworks
--backup-retention-period 7
```

Replace the following placeholders with your specific values:
- `<RDS_INSTANCE_IDENTIFIER>`: A unique name for the new RDS instance.
- `<RDS_INSTANCE_CLASS>`: The instance class for the RDS instance (e.g., `db.t2.micro`).
- `<MASTER_USERNAME>`: The master username for the RDS instance.
- `<MASTER_USER_PASSWORD>`: The master user password for the RDS instance.
- `<VPC_SECURITY_GROUP_ID>`: The VPC security group ID for the RDS instance.
- `<BUCKET_NAME>`: The name of the S3 bucket containing the backup file.
- `<SOURCE_ENGINE_VERSION>`: The PostgreSQL version used on your EC2 instance (e.g., `13.3`).

- `<AWS_REGION>`: The AWS region where the RDS instance is located (e.g., `us-west-2`).
- `<AVAILABILITY_ZONE>`: The availability zone for the RDS instance (e.g., `us-west-2a`).

Verify the Migration

Connect to the AdventureWorks database on the RDS instance using a PostgreSQL client, such as pgAdmin or psql.

Run some SQL queries to verify the tables, data, and other objects have been migrated correctly.

Monitor and Optimize

Monitor the performance and resource usage of your RDS instance and optimize as needed. You can use Amazon CloudWatch to monitor AWS resources and set up alerts for specific events.

Depending on your findings, you may need to:
- Scale the RDS instance vertically by increasing the instance size (CPU, memory, and storage).
- Optimize the PostgreSQL configuration parameters for better performance, such as `shared_buffers`, `effective_cache_size`, and `maintenance_work_mem`.
- Analyze and optimize slow-running queries using the `EXPLAIN` command or other query profiling tools.
- Implement caching, indexing, and partitioning strategies to improve database performance.

By following these steps, you have practically migrated the AdventureWorks database from an Amazon EC2 instance to an Amazon RDS instance. This migration process allows you to take advantage of the managed features of RDS, such as automatic backups, patching, and high availability, while maintaining the performance and flexibility of PostgreSQL.

Recipe#4: Preparing Pgloader to Use with Database

Pgloader is a powerful open-source data migration tool that helps you load data from various sources, including other databases, into PostgreSQL. In this recipe, we'll walk you through the process of preparing Pgloader and making it ready for use with your

AdventureWorks database.

Install Pgloader

Pgloader is available for various platforms, including Linux, macOS, and Windows. Choose the appropriate installation method for your platform:

On Debian-based Linux distributions (Ubuntu, Debian):

```
sudo apt-get update
sudo apt-get install pgloader
```

On macOS (using Homebrew):

```
brew update
brew install pgloader
```

On Windows:
Download the latest Pgloader Windows binary from the GitHub releases page: https://github.com/dimitri/pgloader/releases

Extract the downloaded ZIP file to a directory of your choice.

Add the extracted directory to your system's PATH environment variable.

Verify the Installation

Run the following command in your terminal or command prompt to verify that Pgloader is installed correctly:

```
pgloader --version
```

This should display the version number of Pgloader.

Prepare Source and Target Databases

Ensure that your source database (e.g., MySQL, SQL Server, SQLite) and your target PostgreSQL database are running and accessible. Confirm you have the necessary credentials (username and password) for both databases.

Create Pgloader Command File

A Pgloader command file defines the migration process, including the source and target databases, schema transformations, and data loading options. Create a new text file named pgloader_command_file.load and add the following contents:

```
LOAD DATABASE
    FROM <SOURCE_DB_CONNECTION_STRING>
    INTO <TARGET_DB_CONNECTION_STRING>

 WITH include drop, create tables, create indexes, reset sequences
    data only

 SET maintenance_work_mem to '128MB', work_mem to '12MB', search_path
to 'public'

 CAST type <SOURCE_TYPE> to <TARGET_TYPE> drop typemod

 BEFORE LOAD DO
 $$ create schema if not exists public; $$;
;
```

Replace the placeholders with your specific values:
* <SOURCE_DB_CONNECTION_STRING>: The connection string for your source database (e.g., mysql://user:password@localhost/source_db for MySQL or sqlite:///path/to/sqlite.db for SQLite).
* <TARGET_DB_CONNECTION_STRING>: The connection string for your target PostgreSQL database (e.g., postgresql://user:password@localhost/target_db).
* <SOURCE_TYPE> and <TARGET_TYPE>: If needed, specify any data type casting rules to convert source data types to target data types (e.g., type datetime to timestamptz).

Run the Migration

Execute the following command to start the migration process using the Pgloader command file:

```
pgloader pgloader_command_file.load
```

Pgloader will read the command file and migrate the data from the source database to the target PostgreSQL database. Monitor the progress in the terminal or command prompt, and pay attention to any warnings or errors.

Verify the Migration

Connect to the target PostgreSQL database using a PostgreSQL client, such as pgAdmin or psql.

Run some SQL queries to verify the tables, data, and other objects have been migrated correctly.

Monitor and Optimize

Monitor the performance and resource usage of your PostgreSQL database and optimize as needed. Depending on your findings, you may need to:
- Optimize the PostgreSQL configuration parameters for better performance, such as shared_buffers, effective_cache_size, and maintenance_work_mem.
- Analyze and optimize slow-running queries using the EXPLAIN command or other query profiling tools.
- Implement caching, indexing, and partitioning strategies to improve database performance.
- Scale the PostgreSQL instance vertically by increasing the instance size (CPU, memory, and storage) if hosted on a cloud provider like AWS or Google Cloud Platform.

By following these steps, you have prepared Pgloader and made it ready for use with your AdventureWorks database. Pgloader simplifies the migration process by automatically handling schema and data type conversions, allowing you to focus on optimizing your PostgreSQL database and application performance.

Remember that migrating data from one database system to another can involve various challenges, such as different data types, collations, and indexing strategies. It is essential to thoroughly test the migrated data and application behavior to ensure a smooth transition to PostgreSQL. Additionally, it's crucial to have a rollback plan in case of migration failures or unexpected issues that arise during the migration process.

Recipe#5: Migrating from MySQL to PostgreSQL

In this recipe, we'll walk you through the process of migrating the AdventureWorks database from MySQL to PostgreSQL using Pgloader.

Install Pgloader

Follow the instructions in the previous recipe to install Pgloader on your preferred platform (Linux, macOS, or Windows).

Prepare MySQL and PostgreSQL Environments

Make sure your MySQL server hosting the AdventureWorks database is running and accessible. Ensure you have the necessary credentials (username and password).

Create an empty AdventureWorks database on your PostgreSQL server

CREATE DATABASE adventureworks;

Ensure that the PostgreSQL server hosting the AdventureWorks database is running and accessible. Confirm you have the necessary credentials (username and password).

Create Pgloader Command File

Create a new text file named mysql_to_postgresql.load and add the following contents:

```
LOAD DATABASE
    FROM
mysql://<MYSQL_USERNAME>:<MYSQL_PASSWORD>@<MYSQL_HOST>:<MYSQL_PORT>/adventureworks
    INTO
postgresql://<POSTGRESQL_USERNAME>:<POSTGRESQL_PASSWORD>@<POSTGRESQL_HOST>:<POSTGRESQL_PORT>/adventureworks
```

WITH include drop, create tables, create indexes, reset sequences
    data only

  SET maintenance_work_mem to '128MB', work_mem to '12MB', search_path
to 'public'

CAST type datetime to timestamptz drop typemod,
    type date drop not null using zero-dates-to-null,
    type tinyint to smallint

BEFORE LOAD DO
$$ create schema if not exists public; $$;
;

Replace the placeholders with your specific values:
- <MYSQL_USERNAME>: Your MySQL username.
- <MYSQL_PASSWORD>: Your MySQL password.
- <MYSQL_HOST>: Your MySQL server's hostname or IP address.
- <MYSQL_PORT>: Your MySQL server's port number (default: 3306).
- <POSTGRESQL_USERNAME>: Your PostgreSQL username.
- <POSTGRESQL_PASSWORD>: Your PostgreSQL password.
- <POSTGRESQL_HOST>: Your PostgreSQL server's hostname or IP address.
- <POSTGRESQL_PORT>: Your PostgreSQL server's port number (default: 5432).

Run the Migration

Execute the following command to start the migration process using the Pgloader command file:

pgloader mysql_to_postgresql.load

Pgloader will read the command file and migrate the data from the MySQL database to the PostgreSQL database. Monitor the progress in the terminal or command prompt and pay attention to any warnings or errors.

Verify the Migration

Connect to the AdventureWorks database on the PostgreSQL server using a PostgreSQL client, such as pgAdmin or psql.

Run some SQL queries to verify the tables, data, and other objects have been migrated correctly.

Handle Application Changes

Update your application's database connection settings to use the new PostgreSQL database.

Additionally, you might need to adjust the application code to accommodate differences between MySQL and PostgreSQL, such as:
- SQL syntax differences (e.g., LIMIT and OFFSET vs. FETCH and OFFSET).
- Changes in data types, functions, and operators.
- Different behavior for transactions and locking.

Monitor and Optimize

Monitor the performance and resource usage of your PostgreSQL database and optimize as needed. Depending on your findings, you may need to:

Optimize the PostgreSQL configuration parameters for better performance, such as shared_buffers, effective_cache_size, and maintenance_work_mem.

Analyze and optimize slow-running queries using the EXPLAIN command or other query profiling tools.

By following these steps, you have practically migrated the AdventureWorks database from MySQL to PostgreSQL using Pgloader. Migrating from one database system to another can involve various challenges, such as different data types, collations, and indexing strategies. It is essential to thoroughly test the migrated data and application behavior to ensure a smooth transition to PostgreSQL. Additionally, it's crucial to have a rollback plan in case of migration failures or unexpected issues that arise during the migration process.

Recipe#6: Setting Up Foreign Data Wrapper (FDW)

Foreign Data Wrappers (FDWs) allow you to access and manipulate data stored in remote data sources from within a PostgreSQL database. In the context of database migration, you can use FDWs to access data in the source database (e.g., Oracle, MySQL, SQL Server) and migrate it to PostgreSQL.

Following is how to set up an FDW for migrating the AdventureWorks database to PostgreSQL:

Install Required FDW Extensions

PostgreSQL supports various FDWs out of the box, such as postgres_fdw for accessing PostgreSQL databases and oracle_fdw for accessing Oracle databases. Depending on your source database, you may need to install additional FDW extensions.

Following is an example of installing the mysql_fdw extension for accessing MySQL databases:

```
sudo apt-get update
sudo apt-get install postgresql-contrib-13
sudo apt-get install libmysqlclient-dev
sudo apt-get install postgresql-13-mysql-fdw
```

Create FDW Server

To create an FDW server, you need to define a server object that specifies the connection parameters and options for accessing the remote data source. Following is an example of creating an FDW server for accessing a MySQL database:

```
CREATE SERVER mysql_server
FOREIGN DATA WRAPPER mysql_fdw
OPTIONS (host 'mysql.example.com', port '3306', dbname 'adventureworks',
username 'user', password 'password');
```

Replace the placeholders with your specific values:

- mysql_server: The name of the FDW server object.
- mysql_fdw: The name of the FDW wrapper.
- host, port, dbname, username, password: The connection parameters for accessing the MySQL database.

Create FDW User Mapping

To create an FDW user mapping, you need to specify the remote user credentials for accessing the remote data source. Following is an example of creating an FDW user mapping for the previously created FDW server:

```
CREATE USER MAPPING FOR postgres
SERVER mysql_server
OPTIONS (username 'user', password 'password');
```

Replace the placeholders with your specific values:
- postgres: The name of the local PostgreSQL user who will be accessing the FDW server.
- mysql_server: The name of the FDW server object.
- username, password: The remote user credentials for accessing the MySQL database.

Create FDW Table

To create an FDW table, you need to define a table object that maps to a remote table in the FDW server. Following is an example of creating an FDW table for accessing the salesorderheader table in the AdventureWorks database:

```
CREATE FOREIGN TABLE salesorderheader (
    salesorderid integer,
    revisionnumber integer,
    orderdate date,
    duedate date,
    shipdate date,
    status integer,
    onlineorderflag boolean,
    salesordernumber character varying,
```

```
  purchaseordernumber character varying,
  accountnumber character varying,
  customerid integer,
  salespersonid integer,
  territoryid integer,
  billtoaddressid integer,
  shiptoaddressid integer,
  shipmethodid integer,
  creditcardid integer,
  creditcardapprovalcode character varying,
  currencyrateid integer,
  subtotal numeric(18,2),
  taxamt numeric(18,2),
  freight numeric(18,2),
  totaldue numeric(18,2),
  comment text
)
SERVER mysql_server
OPTIONS (schema_name 'sales', table_name 'salesorderheader');
```

Replace the placeholders with your specific values:
- salesorderheader`: The name of the remote table in the MySQL database.
- sales: The name of the schema in the MySQL database containing the salesorderheader table.

Migrate the Data

To migrate the data from the FDW table to a native PostgreSQL table, execute the following command:

```
INSERT INTO postgres_salesorderheader
SELECT * FROM salesorderheader;
```

Replace postgres_salesorderheader with the name of the native PostgreSQL table you want to migrate the data to.

Verify the Migration

Run some SQL queries to verify the tables, data, and other objects have been migrated correctly.

Handle Application Changes

Update your application's database connection settings to use the new PostgreSQL database.

Additionally, you might need to adjust the application code to accommodate differences between the source database and PostgreSQL, such as:
- SQL syntax differences (e.g., LIMIT and OFFSET vs. FETCH and OFFSET).
- Changes in data types, functions, and operators.
- Different behavior for transactions and locking.

By following these steps, you have practically migrated the AdventureWorks database to PostgreSQL using FDW. Migrating from one database system to another can involve various challenges, such as different data types, collations, and indexing strategies. It is essential to thoroughly test the migrated data and application behavior to ensure a smooth transition to PostgreSQL. Additionally, it's crucial to have a rollback plan in case of migration failures or unexpected issues that arise during the migration process.

CHAPTER 5: WAL, AUTOVACUUM & ARCHIVELOG

Recipe#1: Enable and Disable Archive Mode

To enable or disable the Archive mode for a PostgreSQL database, you need to have an existing PostgreSQL database and server. In this case, I will provide you with general instructions on how to enable or disable Archive mode for a PostgreSQL database, as the link provided does not have a direct impact on the Archive mode.

Archive mode in PostgreSQL refers to the Write-Ahead Logging (WAL) mechanism, which logs all modifications made to the database. When Archive mode is enabled, completed WAL files are stored for later usage, allowing Point-In-Time Recovery (PITR) or replication.

To enable/disable Archive mode, follow these steps:

Update postgresql.conf Configuration File

This file is usually located in the PostgreSQL data directory, which can be found by running the following command:

SHOW data_directory;

Open the postgresql.conf file with your preferred text editor.

Enable Archive Mode

To enable Archive mode, find and modify the following parameters in the postgresql.conf file:

wal_level = replica
archive_mode = on
archive_command = 'cp %p /path/to/archive/directory/%f'

Replace /path/to/archive/directory with the directory where you want to store archived WAL files. Confirm the PostgreSQL user has write access to this directory.

Disable Archive Mode

To disable Archive mode, find and modify the following parameters in the postgresql.conf file:

wal_level = replica
archive_mode = off

You can comment out or remove the archive_command line as it is not used when Archive mode is disabled.

Restart PostgreSQL Server

After making the changes, you need to restart the PostgreSQL server for the changes to take effect. You can do this using the appropriate command for your operating system.

For example, on Linux systems, you can use:

sudo systemctl restart postgresql

On Windows systems, you can restart the PostgreSQL service from the Services management console or use the following command in the Command Prompt (running as Administrator):

net stop postgresql && net start postgresql

Now you have enabled or disabled Archive mode for your PostgreSQL database. Please note that enabling or disabling Archive mode is a global setting that affects all databases on the PostgreSQL server.

Recipe#2: WAL Compression Option for Space Management

Write-Ahead Logging (WAL) compression is an option in PostgreSQL that helps reduce the storage space required for WAL files. By enabling WAL compression, PostgreSQL compresses the main data portion of WAL records, which reduces the amount of I/O and storage needed to maintain the WAL. This can improve write performance and help manage space, especially for larger databases.

To enable WAL compression, follow these steps:

Locate postgresql.conf Configuration File

As mentioned in the previous recipe, the postgresql.conf file is usually located in the PostgreSQL data directory. You can find the location by running the following command:

SHOW data_directory;

Open the postgresql.conf file with your preferred text editor.

Enable WAL Compression

Find the wal_compression parameter in the postgresql.conf file. Uncomment the line if it's commented (remove the '#' at the beginning of the line) and set it to on:

wal_compression = on

Save the changes to the postgresql.conf file.

Restart PostgreSQL Server

After making the changes, you need to restart the PostgreSQL server for the changes to take effect. You can do this using the appropriate command for your operating system.

For example, on Linux systems, you can use:

sudo systemctl restart postgresql

On Windows systems, you can restart the PostgreSQL service from the Services management console or use the following command in the Command Prompt (running as Administrator):

net stop postgresql && net start postgresql

After completing these steps, WAL compression will be enabled, and PostgreSQL will compress the main data portion of new WAL records. This will help save storage space and improve write performance. Keep in mind that compression comes with some CPU overhead, but it is typically a reasonable trade-off for the space savings and I/O reduction achieved.

Recipe#3: Configure WAL Performance Parameter

To configure and manage Write-Ahead Logging (WAL) performance in a PostgreSQL database, you can adjust several parameters in the postgresql.conf file. Tuning these parameters helps balance the trade-offs between write performance, recovery time, and replication lag. Following is a practical recipe on how to configure and manage these parameters:

Locate postgresql.conf Configuration File

As mentioned before, the postgresql.conf file is usually located in the PostgreSQL data directory. You can find the location by running the following command:

```
SHOW data_directory;
```

Open the postgresql.conf file with your preferred text editor.

Configure WAL Performance Parameters

There are several parameters you can adjust to manage WAL performance.

Here are some of the most important ones:
- wal_level: Determines the level of detail written to the WAL. Higher levels increase the amount of information logged, which can affect performance but may be required for certain features, like logical replication or point-in-time recovery. Valid options are minimal, replica, and logical. For most cases, the default value replica is a good balance.

```
wal_level = replica
```

- wal_buffers: Specifies the number of disk-page buffers used for WAL data. Increasing this value can improve write performance but uses more shared memory. The default is -1, which sets the size to 1/32 of shared_buffers or 8MB, whichever is smaller. You can experiment with larger values (e.g., 16MB) to see if it improves performance.

```
wal_buffers = 16MB
```

- checkpoint_timeout: Determines the maximum time between automatic checkpoints. Increasing this value reduces the frequency of checkpoints, which can improve write performance but may increase recovery time. The default is 5 minutes. You can try increasing it to 10 minutes and monitor the impact on performance and recovery time.

checkpoint_timeout = 10min

- max_wal_size: Specifies the amount of WAL that can be generated between checkpoints. When this limit is reached, a checkpoint will be triggered. Increasing this value can improve write performance but may increase recovery time. The default is 1GB. You can try increasing it to 2GB and monitor the impact on performance and recovery time.

max_wal_size = 2GB

- min_wal_size: Specifies the minimum amount of WAL space reserved for the system. The system tries to maintain this much space for WAL at all times. The default is 80MB. Increasing this value can help avoid running out of WAL space during high-load periods.

min_wal_size = 128MB

- synchronous_commit: Controls whether transaction commits must wait for WAL records to be flushed to disk. Disabling synchronous commit (off) can improve write performance but may result in data loss in case of a crash. The default is on. Use this setting with caution and only if you can afford potential data loss.

synchronous_commit = off

Save the changes to the postgresql.conf file.

Restart PostgreSQL Server

After making the changes, you need to restart the PostgreSQL server for the changes to take effect. You can do this using the appropriate command for your operating system.

For example, on Linux systems, you can use:

```
sudo systemctl restart postgresql
```

On Windows systems, you can restart the PostgreSQL service from the Services management console or use the following command in the Command Prompt (running as Administrator):

```
net stop postgresql && net start
```

Monitor WAL Performance

After making the changes and restarting the server, monitor the performance to see if the changes had the desired effect. You can use various tools to monitor WAL performance, such as pg_stat_replication, pg_stat_archiver, and pg_stat_bgwriter.

For example, to check the replication lag of a replica, run the following command:

```
SELECT client_addr, pg_xlog_location_diff(sent_location, replay_location) AS
replication_lag
FROM pg_stat_replication;
```

To check the status of the WAL archiver, run the following command:

```
SELECT archived_count, last_archived_wal, last_archived_time
FROM pg_stat_archiver;
```

To check the number of buffers written by the background writer, run the following command:

```
SELECT checkpoints_timed, checkpoints_req, buffers_checkpoint,
buffers_clean, buffers_backend
FROM pg_stat_bgwriter;
```

Monitor the performance over time and adjust the parameters as needed to achieve the desired balance between write performance, recovery time, and replication lag.

The above aforesaid steps are the recommended ones to configure and manage WAL performance in a PostgreSQL database. Keep in mind that tuning WAL performance requires a good understanding of the workload and system characteristics, and should be done with caution. Always test changes in a non-production environment before applying them to production.

Recipe#4: Administer Continuous Archiving

Continuous Archiving is the process of continuously copying Write-Ahead Log (WAL) files to a separate storage location, which can then be used for Point-In-Time Recovery (PITR) or for replication purposes. PostgreSQL 15 includes several improvements and new features for Continuous Archiving, including the ability to use multiple archive destinations and to specify a custom script to manage archiving.

Here are the steps to administer Continuous Archiving in PostgreSQL 15:

Configure Archive Command

In PostgreSQL 15, you can specify a custom script to manage archiving by setting the archive_command parameter in the postgresql.conf file. The script should copy WAL files to a designated archive destination, such as a remote server or cloud storage.

For example, to use rsync to copy WAL files to a remote server, you can set the archive_command parameter to:

```
archive_command = 'rsync %p username@remotehost:/path/to/archive/%f'
```

This command will copy the WAL file specified by %p to the remote server, using the username username and storing the file in the /path/to/archive directory with the same filename as the WAL file (%f).

Configure Archive Mode

To enable Continuous Archiving, you need to set the archive_mode parameter to on in the postgresql.conf file:

```
archive_mode = on
```

This parameter tells PostgreSQL to archive WAL files as they are written to disk.

Specify Archive Destinations

PostgreSQL 15 allows you to specify multiple archive destinations, which can be useful for redundancy or load balancing. To specify multiple archive destinations, you can set the archive_destinations parameter in the postgresql.conf file:

```
archive_destinations =
'/path/to/archive1/,username@remotehost:/path/to/archive2/'
```

This parameter specifies two archive destinations: a local directory (/path/to/archive1/) and a remote server (username@remotehost:/path/to/archive2/). The two destinations are separated by a comma.

Restart PostgreSQL

After making changes to the postgresql.conf file, you need to restart PostgreSQL to apply the changes:

```
systemctl restart postgresql-15
```

This command restarts PostgreSQL 15 on a systemd-based system.

Test Archiving

To test archiving, you can create a new database and insert some data. Then, create a checkpoint by running the following command:

```
SELECT pg_create_checkpoint();
```

This command creates a checkpoint, which flushes all changes to disk and generates a new WAL file.

Check that the WAL file has been archived by checking the archive destination(s) specified in the archive_command and archive_destinations parameters.

Monitor Archiving

You can monitor archiving using various system views and functions, such as pg_stat_archiver and pg_switch_wal. These views provide information about the status of archiving, such as the number of WAL files archived and the last archived WAL file.

For example, to check the status of archiving, run the following command:

```
SELECT *
FROM pg_stat_archiver;
```

This command shows the status of archiving, including the last archived WAL file and the number of WAL files waiting to be archived.

The above aforesaid steps are the recommended ones to administer Continuous Archiving in PostgreSQL 15. Continuous Archiving is an important tool for ensuring data durability and high availability in PostgreSQL databases.

Recipe#5: Using Remote WAL Archive Options

Remote WAL archiving is the process of copying Write-Ahead Log (WAL) files from a primary PostgreSQL server to a remote server for disaster recovery purposes. This is typically done using a tool like rsync or scp to copy the files over the network. PostgreSQL provides several options for working with remote WAL archiving, including specifying the remote archive location, setting up SSH keys for secure file transfer, and using compression to reduce network traffic.

Following are the steps to work with remote WAL archive options in PostgreSQL:

Configure Archive Command

To specify the remote archive location, you can set the archive_command parameter in the postgresql.conf file to a command that copies WAL files to the remote server. For example, to use rsync to copy WAL files to a remote server with IP address 192.0.2.1, you can set the archive_command parameter to:

```
archive_command = 'rsync %p user@192.0.2.1:/path/to/archive/%f'
```

This command will copy the WAL file specified by %p to the remote server, using the username user and storing the file in the /path/to/archive directory with the same filename as the WAL file (%f).

Setup SSH Keys

To secure the file transfer, it is recommended to set up SSH keys for authentication. This allows the primary server to authenticate with the remote server without requiring a password.

First, create a public/private key pair on the primary server by running the following command:

```
ssh-keygen
```

This command creates a public/private key pair in the ~/.ssh directory.

Then, copy the public key to the remote server by running the following command:

```
ssh-copy-id user@192.0.2.1
```

This command copies the public key to the remote server and adds it to the authorized_keys file, allowing the primary server to authenticate without a password.

Test Archiving

To test remote WAL archiving, you can create a new database and insert some data. Then, create a checkpoint by running the following command:

```
SELECT pg_create_checkpoint();
```

This command creates a checkpoint, which flushes all changes to disk and generates a new WAL file.

Check that the WAL file has been archived on the remote server by checking the archive destination specified in the archive_command parameter.

Enable Compression (optional)

To reduce network traffic and improve performance, you can enable compression for remote WAL archiving by adding the -z option to the rsync command in the archive_command parameter:

archive_command = 'rsync -z %p user@192.0.2.1:/path/to/archive/%f'

This command enables compression for the file transfer, which can help reduce the amount of data transferred over the network.

The above aforesaid steps are the recommended ones to work with remote WAL archive options in PostgreSQL. Remote WAL archiving is an important tool for disaster recovery and high availability in PostgreSQL databases.

Recipe#6: Exploring Vacuum Process

In PostgreSQL, the VACUUM process is used to reclaim storage space occupied by dead rows and to improve query performance. When a row is deleted or updated, the old version of the row is not immediately removed from the table. Instead, it becomes a dead row, which is still visible to other transactions but cannot be accessed by any new transactions. These dead rows consume disk space and may cause performance issues if they accumulate over time.

The VACUUM process scans the table and removes dead rows, freeing up storage space and improving query performance. In addition to removing dead rows, VACUUM also reclaims unused space within the table and updates the visibility information of rows to improve query planning.

To perform a VACUUM on the adventureworks database, you can use the following command:

VACUUM FULL;

This command performs a full VACUUM of all tables in the database, which may take some time for larger databases. It removes dead rows and reclaims unused space within the tables, which can improve performance and reduce disk space usage.

Note that VACUUM can cause some level of locking, and may affect concurrent access to the tables being vacuumed. For this reason, it is recommended to schedule regular VACUUM operations during periods of low database activity.

In addition to the VACUUM process, PostgreSQL provides several other tools for managing database storage and performance, such as pg_dump for backing up and restoring databases, and pg_repack for optimizing table storage. These tools can be useful for managing the adventureworks database and ensuring its performance and stability.

Recipe#7: Estimate Transaction Log Size

To estimate the transaction log size for a PostgreSQL database, you can use the following SQL statement:

```
SELECT
  (SELECT sum(pg_database_size(datname)) FROM pg_database WHERE
datname = 'adventureworks') / current_setting('wal_segment_size')::numeric *
current_setting('wal_retention_bytes')::numeric /
current_setting('wal_segment_size')::numeric AS log_size;
```

This SQL statement calculates the estimated size of the transaction log for the adventureworks database, based on the current database size and the configuration settings for the transaction log size.

The calculation is based on the following factors:
- The size of the database, obtained using pg_database_size()
- The size of each WAL segment, obtained using current_setting('wal_segment_size')
- The retention period of the transaction log, obtained using current_setting('wal_retention_bytes')
- The result is expressed in units of WAL segments, which can be used to determine the disk space required for the transaction log.

This is an estimation, and the actual transaction log size may vary depending on the workload and usage patterns of the database. It is recommended to monitor the transaction log size regularly and adjust the configuration settings as needed to avoid running out of disk space.

To run the SQL statement, you can use any PostgreSQL client tool, such as psql or PgAdmin. Following is an example of how to run the SQL statement using psql:

Open a terminal window and connect to the adventureworks database using psql:

```
psql -d adventureworks
```

Enter the SQL statement in the psql prompt:

```
SELECT
  (SELECT sum(pg_database_size(datname)) FROM pg_database WHERE
datname = 'adventureworks') / current_setting('wal_segment_size')::numeric *
current_setting('wal_retention_bytes')::numeric /
current_setting('wal_segment_size')::numeric AS log_size;
```

Press Enter to execute the SQL statement.

The result will be displayed in the psql prompt, showing the estimated size of the
transaction log in WAL segments.

This is how you can use an SQL statement to estimate the transaction log size for a
PostgreSQL database.

Recipe#8: Debug PostgreSQL Autovaccum

Autovacuum is a process in PostgreSQL that automatically reclaims storage space and
optimizes table performance. However, sometimes autovacuum may not work as expected,
leading to performance issues and disk space usage problems. Here are the steps to debug
autovacuum problems in PostgreSQL for the adventureworks database:

Check Autovacuum Settings

The first step is to check the autovacuum settings for the adventureworks database. You
can do this by running the following query:

```
SELECT name, setting FROM pg_settings WHERE name LIKE
'autovacuum%';
```

This query shows the current values of autovacuum-related parameters, such as
autovacuum_vacuum_scale_factor,   autovacuum_analyze_scale_factor,   and
autovacuum_freeze_max_age.

Check that the settings are appropriate for the workload and database size.

Check Autovacuum Logs

Autovacuum logs can provide valuable information about the behavior of the autovacuum process, including the tables being vacuumed and the reasons for vacuuming. Check the PostgreSQL log files for autovacuum messages, such as:

```
LOG: automatic vacuum of table "public.orders": index scans: 1
```

This message shows that the autovacuum process vacuumed the orders table in the public schema, and performed one index scan.

Monitor Table Statistics

PostgreSQL provides several system views for monitoring table statistics, such as pg_stat_all_tables and pg_stat_user_tables. These views provide information about table sizes, dead row counts, and other performance metrics. Check these views to identify tables that may require vacuuming or analyzing.

For example, to list tables that have a high number of dead rows, you can run the following query:

```
SELECT schemaname, relname, n_dead_tup
FROM pg_stat_user_tables
WHERE n_dead_tup > 1000;
```

This query shows tables in the user schema that have more than 1000 dead rows.

Manually Vacuum Tables

If autovacuum is not working as expected, you can manually vacuum tables using the VACUUM command. For example, to vacuum the orders table in the public schema, you can run the following command:

```
VACUUM public.orders;
```

This command vacuums the orders table, removing dead rows and reclaiming unused space.

Increase Autovacuum Settings

If autovacuum is not keeping up with the workload, you may need to increase the autovacuum settings to vacuum tables more frequently or more aggressively. You can do this by changing the autovacuum_vacuum_scale_factor and autovacuum_analyze_scale_factor parameters in the postgresql.conf file, or by using the ALTER TABLE command to set per-table autovacuum settings.

For example, to set the autovacuum_vacuum_scale_factor parameter to 0.05 for the adventureworks database, you can run the following command:

```
ALTER DATABASE adventureworks SET autovacuum_vacuum_scale_factor = 0.05;
```

This command sets the autovacuum_vacuum_scale_factor parameter to 0.05, which causes autovacuum to vacuum tables more frequently.

The above aforesaid steps are the recommended ones to debug autovacuum problems in PostgreSQL for the adventureworks database. By monitoring autov

Recipe#9: Delete PostgreSQL Archive Logs

In PostgreSQL, archive logs are used for point-in-time recovery and replication. However, over time these logs can accumulate and take up a significant amount of disk space. To delete archive logs for the adventureworks database, you can use the following steps:

Determine the Archive Directory Location

To delete archive logs, you need to determine the location of the archive directory for the adventureworks database. You can check the value of the archive_command parameter in the postgresql.conf file to determine the directory location. For example, if the archive_command parameter is set to:

```
archive_command = 'cp %p /mnt/server/archives/%f'
```

This indicates that archive logs are stored in the /mnt/server/archives directory.

Determine the Retention Policy

The retention policy determines how long archive logs should be retained before they are eligible for deletion. You can check the value of the archive_timeout parameter in the postgresql.conf file to determine the retention policy. For example, if the archive_timeout parameter is set to:

archive_timeout = 86400

This indicates that archive logs should be retained for 24 hours (86400 seconds) before they are eligible for deletion.

Identify Archive Logs to Delete

Once you have determined the archive directory location and retention policy, you can identify archive logs that are eligible for deletion. To do this, you can list the contents of the archive directory and filter the list based on the retention policy. For example, to list archive logs in the /mnt/server/archives directory that are older than 24 hours, you can run the following command:

find /mnt/server/archives -type f -mtime +1

This command lists all files (-type f) in the /mnt/server/archives directory that were last modified more than 1 day ago (-mtime +1).

Delete Archive Logs

Once you have identified archive logs that are eligible for deletion, you can delete them using the rm command. For example, to delete all archive logs in the /mnt/server/archives directory that are older than 24 hours, you can run the following command:

find /mnt/server/archives -type f -mtime +1 -delete

This command deletes all files (-type f) in the /mnt/server/archives directory that were last modified more than 1 day ago (-mtime +1).

The above aforesaid steps are the recommended ones to delete archive logs for the adventureworks database in PostgreSQL. Note that deleting archive logs can affect the ability to perform point-in-time recovery and replication, so it is important to carefully manage archive log retention and deletion policies.

CHAPTER 6: PARTITIONING AND SHARDING STRATEGIES

Recipe#1: Setup Partitioning in PostgreSQL 15

Partitioning is a technique used in PostgreSQL to improve query performance and manage large tables by dividing them into smaller, more manageable partitions. Each partition is essentially a smaller table with its own set of indexes and storage characteristics, allowing queries to be processed more efficiently and reducing the risk of table bloat.

Below is how to set up partitioning in PostgreSQL 15 for the adventureworks database:

Choose Partitioning Strategy

There are several partitioning strategies available in PostgreSQL, such as range partitioning, list partitioning, and hash partitioning. Choose a partitioning strategy that is appropriate for the data and queries in the adventureworks database.

Create Partitioned Table

To create a partitioned table in PostgreSQL, use the CREATE TABLE command with the PARTITION BY clause. For example, to create a partitioned table for orders based on the order date, you can run the following command:

```
CREATE TABLE orders (
  id serial PRIMARY KEY,
  order_date date NOT NULL,
  customer_id integer NOT NULL,
  ...
)
PARTITION BY RANGE (order_date);
```

This command creates a partitioned table for orders, partitioned by the order_date column using range partitioning.

Create Partitions

Once the partitioned table is created, you can create partitions by using the CREATE TABLE command with the PARTITION OF clause. For example, to create a partition for orders placed in January 2023, you can run the following command:

CREATE TABLE orders_202301 PARTITION OF orders
FOR VALUES FROM ('2023-01-01') TO ('2023-02-01');

This command creates a partition for orders placed in January 2023, with a range of '2023-01-01' to '2023-02-01'.

Index Partitions

Indexes can be created on each partition separately or on the partitioned table as a whole. Depending on the partitioning strategy and the queries being executed, it may be more efficient to create indexes on each partition separately. For example, to create an index on the customer_id column for the orders_202301 partition, you can run the following command:

CREATE INDEX orders_202301_customer_id_idx ON orders_202301
(customer_id);

This command creates an index on the customer_id column for the orders_202301 partition.

Insert Data

Once the partitions are created, you can insert data into the partitioned table as usual. PostgreSQL will automatically route the data to the appropriate partition based on the partitioning strategy.

Optimize Partitions

Over time, the performance of the partitions may degrade due to bloat and other factors. To optimize partitions, you can use tools such as VACUUM and pg_repack to reclaim storage space and reorganize the data within the partitions.

The above aforesaid steps are the recommended ones to set up partitioning in PostgreSQL 15 for the adventureworks database. Note that partitioning can significantly improve query performance and manageability for large tables, but it requires careful planning and ongoing maintenance to ensure optimal performance.

Recipe#2: Vertical & Horizontal Partitioning

In addition to regular partitioning, PostgreSQL also supports vertical and horizontal partitioning to further improve query performance and manageability for large tables.

Vertical partitioning involves splitting a table into multiple tables based on columns, with each table containing a subset of columns. This can be useful when certain columns are accessed more frequently than others, or when certain columns contain large amounts of data that can be stored separately for improved query performance. To achieve vertical partitioning in PostgreSQL, you can use the CREATE TABLE command to create separate tables for each subset of columns, and use the JOIN operation to combine the results of multiple tables.

Horizontal partitioning involves splitting a table into multiple tables based on rows, with each table containing a subset of rows. This can be useful when a table contains a large number of rows that are accessed infrequently, or when certain rows can be logically grouped together for improved query performance. To achieve horizontal partitioning in PostgreSQL, you can use the regular partitioning techniques described in the previous solution.

For the adventureworks database, here are examples of how to achieve vertical and horizontal partitioning:

Vertical Partitioning

Suppose the orders table in the adventureworks database contains a large amount of data in the order_details column, which is rarely accessed. To vertically partition the orders table based on this column, you can create a separate table for the order_details column, and join the two tables as needed. Following is an example of how to do this:

```
CREATE TABLE orders (
  id serial PRIMARY KEY,
  order_date date NOT NULL,
  customer_id integer NOT NULL,
  ...
);

CREATE TABLE order_details (
```

```
  id serial PRIMARY KEY,
  order_id integer REFERENCES orders (id),
  details jsonb NOT NULL
);
```

This command creates two tables: orders and order_details. The orders table contains the columns that are frequently accessed, while the order_details table contains the order_id and details columns.

To retrieve the order_details for a specific order, you can join the two tables as follows:

```
SELECT orders.*, order_details.details
FROM orders
JOIN order_details ON orders.id = order_details.order_id
WHERE orders.id = 123;
```

Horizontal Partitioning

Suppose the orders table in the adventureworks database contains a large number of rows, making queries slow and inefficient. To horizontally partition the orders table based on the order_date column, you can create separate tables for each partition, and use a parent table to route queries to the appropriate partition. Following is an example of how to do this:

```
CREATE TABLE orders (
  id serial PRIMARY KEY,
  order_date date NOT NULL,
  customer_id integer NOT NULL,
  ...
);

CREATE TABLE orders_2022 (
  CHECK (order_date >= '2022-01-01' AND order_date < '2023-01-01')
) INHERITS (orders);
```

```sql
CREATE TABLE orders_2023 (
  CHECK (order_date >= '2023-01-01' AND order_date < '2024-01-01')
) INHERITS (orders);

CREATE TABLE orders_2024 (
  CHECK (order_date >= '2024-01-01' AND order_date < '2025-01-01')
) INHERITS (orders);
```

This command creates three tables: orders, orders_2022, orders_2023, and orders_2024. Each partition contains a subset of rows based on the order_date column. The INHERITS clause indicates that each child table inherits the structure of the parent table.

To insert data into the appropriate partition, you can specify the partition name in the INSERT statement. For example:

```sql
INSERT INTO orders_2022 (order_date, customer_id, ...)
VALUES ('2022-01-01', 123, ...);
```

To retrieve data from the partitioned table, you can query the parent table as usual. PostgreSQL will automatically route the query to the appropriate partition based on the CHECK constraints defined in each child table.

```sql
SELECT *
FROM orders
WHERE order_date >= '2022-01-01' AND order_date < '2023-01-01';
```

This command retrieves all rows from the orders table where the order_date is in the year 2022.

The above aforesaid steps are the recommended ones to achieve vertical and horizontal partitioning in PostgreSQL for the adventureworks database. By partitioning large tables, you can improve query performance and manageability, while also reducing the risk of table bloat and other performance issues.

Recipe#3: Perform Attaching, Detaching and Drop Partition

In PostgreSQL, partitions can be attached and detached from a partitioned table dynamically, allowing for flexible management of data over time. Following is how to perform attaching, detaching, and dropping partitions with PostgreSQL 15 for the adventureworks database:

Attaching Partition

To attach a new partition to a partitioned table, you can use the ALTER TABLE command with the ATTACH PARTITION clause. For example, to attach a partition for orders placed in February 2023, you can run the following command:

```
ALTER TABLE orders
ATTACH PARTITION orders_202302
FOR VALUES FROM ('2023-02-01') TO ('2023-03-01');
```

This command attaches a new partition named orders_202302 to the orders table, with a range of '2023-02-01' to '2023-03-01'.

Detaching Partition

To detach a partition from a partitioned table, you can use the ALTER TABLE command with the DETACH PARTITION clause. For example, to detach the orders_202302 partition from the orders table, you can run the following command:

```
ALTER TABLE orders
DETACH PARTITION orders_202302;
```

This command detaches the orders_202302 partition from the orders table.

Dropping Partition

To drop a partition completely from the database, you can use the DROP TABLE command. For example, to drop the orders_202302 partition from the database, you can run the following command:

DROP TABLE orders_202302;

This command drops the orders_202302 partition from the database.

Note that when dropping a partition, you should ensure that any data contained in the partition is no longer needed or has been moved to another partition. Dropping a partition will permanently delete all data contained in the partition, so it should be done with care.

The above aforesaid steps are the recommended ones to perform attaching, detaching, and dropping partitions with PostgreSQL 15 for the adventureworks database. By dynamically managing partitions, you can improve data management and performance for large tables over time.

Recipe#4: Tables Partitioning using Table Inheritance

In PostgreSQL, it is possible to partition an existing table by using table inheritance. Table inheritance allows you to create a child table that inherits the structure of a parent table, while also adding additional columns or constraints. Following is how to use table inheritance for table partitioning in the adventureworks database:

Create Parent Table

To partition an existing table, you first need to create a parent table that will serve as the basis for the child tables. For example, to partition the orders table in the adventureworks database by month, you can create a parent table called orders_parent with the following command:

```
CREATE TABLE orders_parent (
  id serial PRIMARY KEY,
  order_date date NOT NULL,
  customer_id integer NOT NULL,
  ...
);
```

This command creates a parent table called orders_parent with the same structure as the orders table.

Create Child Tables

Once the parent table is created, you can create child tables that inherit its structure. To create a child table for orders placed in January 2023, you can use the following command:

```
CREATE TABLE orders_202301 (
  CHECK (order_date >= '2023-01-01' AND order_date < '2023-02-01')
) INHERITS (orders_parent);
```

This command creates a child table called orders_202301 that inherits the structure of the orders_parent table. The CHECK constraint defines the range of order_date values that should be stored in this partition.

You can create additional child tables for each partition as needed, using the same structure as the parent table.

Index Child Tables

Indexes can be created on each child table separately or on the parent table as a whole. Depending on the partitioning strategy and the queries being executed, it may be more efficient to create indexes on each child table separately. For example, to create an index on the customer_id column for the orders_202301 partition, you can run the following command:

```
CREATE INDEX orders_202301_customer_id_idx ON orders_202301
(customer_id);
```

This command creates an index on the customer_id column for the orders_202301 partition.

Insert Data

Once the child tables are created, you can insert data into the partitioned table as usual. PostgreSQL will automatically route the data to the appropriate partition based on the partitioning strategy.

Optimize Partitions

Over time, the performance of the partitions may degrade due to bloat and other factors.

To optimize partitions, you can use tools such as VACUUM and pg_repack to reclaim storage space and reorganize the data within the partitions.

The above aforesaid steps are the recommended ones to use table inheritance for table partitioning in the adventureworks database. Note that table inheritance can be a powerful technique for partitioning existing tables, but it requires careful planning and ongoing maintenance to ensure optimal performance.

Recipe#5: Implement Automatic Partition

In PostgreSQL 10 and later versions, the concept of declarative partitioning was introduced, which allows for automatic partitioning of data based on predefined rules. This can simplify the process of managing large tables by automatically creating and managing partitions, based on predefined rules. Following is how to implement automatic partitioning in PostgreSQL 15 for the adventureworks database:

Create Partitioned Table

To create a partitioned table, you can use the CREATE TABLE command with the PARTITION BY clause, and specify the partitioning strategy. For example, to partition the orders table in the adventureworks database by month, you can run the following command:

```
CREATE TABLE orders (
  id serial PRIMARY KEY,
  order_date date NOT NULL,
  customer_id integer NOT NULL,
  ...
)
PARTITION BY RANGE (order_date);
```

This command creates a partitioned table called orders with the same structure as the orders table, and specifies that the table should be partitioned based on the order_date column.

Create Partitions Automatically

Once the partitioned table is created, you can create partitions automatically based on predefined rules using the CREATE TABLE command. For example, to create a partition for orders placed in January 2023, you can run the following command:

```
CREATE TABLE orders_202301 PARTITION OF orders
FOR VALUES FROM ('2023-01-01') TO ('2023-02-01');
```

This command creates a partition called orders_202301 for the orders table, based on the order_date values in the range of '2023-01-01' to '2023-02-01'.

You can create additional partitions as needed, and PostgreSQL will automatically route data to the appropriate partition based on the partitioning strategy.

The above aforesaid steps are the recommended ones to implement automatic partitioning in PostgreSQL 15 for the adventureworks database. Automatic partitioning can simplify the process of managing large tables, and help ensure optimal performance by automatically creating and managing partitions based on predefined rules.

Recipe#6: Partition Pruning

Partition pruning is a technique used by PostgreSQL to speed up queries on partitioned tables by eliminating partitions that do not contain relevant data. This is achieved by analyzing the query conditions and identifying which partitions are likely to contain relevant data, and then only scanning those partitions during query execution. Partition pruning can greatly improve query performance on large partitioned tables, by reducing the amount of data that needs to be scanned.

Following is how to make partition pruning useful for the adventureworks database:

Define Partition Ranges

To enable partition pruning, you first need to define the partition ranges for the table. This can be done using the CREATE TABLE command with the PARTITION BY clause, as described in the previous solution.

Index Partitions

Indexes can be created on each partition separately or on the partitioned table as a whole, as described in the previous solution. Indexes can greatly improve query performance by allowing PostgreSQL to quickly locate relevant data within each partition.

Optimize Partitions

As with regular tables, partitions may need to be optimized over time to ensure optimal performance. Tools such as VACUUM and pg_repack can be used to reclaim storage space and reorganize the data within the partitions.

Use Partition Key in Queries

To take advantage of partition pruning, queries must be written to include the partition key in the WHERE clause. For example, to retrieve all orders placed in January 2023, you can run the following command:

```
SELECT *
FROM orders
WHERE order_date >= '2023-01-01' AND order_date < '2023-02-01';
```

This command includes the order_date column in the WHERE clause, which allows PostgreSQL to identify the relevant partition(s) and only scan those partitions during query execution. Without the partition key in the WHERE clause, PostgreSQL would need to scan all partitions, which would be much slower for large tables.

By following these steps, you can make partition pruning useful for the adventureworks database, and greatly improve query performance on large partitioned tables.

Recipe#7: Run Declarative Partition

To run declarative partitioning on the adventureworks database using PostgreSQL 15, you can follow these steps:

Create Child Tables

Use the CREATE TABLE statement with the PARTITION OF clause to create the child tables that will inherit from the partitioned table. For example, to create a child table called orders_january that will hold all orders from January 2023, you could use the following statement:

```
CREATE TABLE orders_january PARTITION OF orders_partitioned
FOR VALUES FROM ('2023-01-01') TO ('2023-02-01');
```

This statement creates the orders_january table as a child table of orders_partitioned and specifies that it should hold all orders with an order_date between January 1, 2023, and February 1, 2023.

You can create additional child tables as needed for the other months.

Add Constraints to Child Tables

Use the ALTER TABLE statement to add constraints to the child tables as needed. For example, to add a foreign key constraint to the orders_january table, you could use the following statement:

```
ALTER TABLE orders_january ADD CONSTRAINT
orders_january_customer_fk
  FOREIGN KEY (customer_id) REFERENCES customers(id);
```

This statement adds a foreign key constraint to the customer_id column in the orders_january table that references the id column in the customers table.

Optimize Partitions

As with any table, partitions may need to be optimized over time to ensure optimal performance. Use the VACUUM and pg_repack tools to reclaim storage space and reorganize the data within the partitions.

With these steps, you can run declarative partitioning on the adventureworks database using PostgreSQL 15.

Recipe#8: Administer Performance with Table Partitioning

Table partitioning in PostgreSQL can be a powerful technique for improving database performance, especially for very large tables. Here are some tips for administering performance with table partitioning in the adventureworks database:

Choose Appropriate Partitioning Strategy

There are several different partitioning strategies available in PostgreSQL, including range partitioning, list partitioning, and hash partitioning. The best strategy for your database will depend on the characteristics of your data and your query workload. It's important to choose an appropriate partitioning strategy that will enable efficient partition pruning and avoid excessive partition overlap.

Use Appropriate Partition Ranges

When defining partition ranges, it's important to choose appropriate ranges that will allow for efficient partition pruning. For example, if you're partitioning a table by date, it may be best to use monthly partitions rather than daily partitions, depending on the size of the table and the typical query workload.

Optimize Partition Size

It's important to optimize the size of each partition to balance query performance with storage efficiency. If partitions are too small, there may be too much overhead associated with managing them. If partitions are too large, query performance may suffer due to excessive partition overlap.

Monitor Partition Size and Bloat

Regularly monitor the size and bloat of partitions to ensure optimal performance. Use tools such as VACUUM and pg_repack to reclaim storage space and reorganize the data within the partitions as needed.

Use Appropriate Indexing

Ensure that each partition is appropriately indexed to support efficient query execution. This may require creating separate indexes on each partition, or using a single index on the partitioned table as a whole, depending on the query workload.

Test and Optimize Queries

Test queries to ensure that they are taking advantage of partition pruning and that performance is optimized. Make adjustments to the partitioning strategy or indexing as needed to ensure optimal query performance.

By following these tips, you can administer performance with table partitioning in the adventureworks database and ensure that queries execute efficiently on very large tables.

Recipe#9: Setting up Shard with FWD

Setting up sharding with FWD (Flexible Web Data) in PostgreSQL involves partitioning data across multiple servers or instances, typically based on a specific key or range of keys. Here are the steps to set up sharding with FWD for the adventureworks database:

Choose Sharding Key

The sharding key is the column or set of columns used to partition the data across multiple servers or instances. For example, if you want to shard the orders table in the adventureworks database, you could use the customer_id column as the sharding key.

Create Shards

Each shard represents a separate database instance or server. Use the CREATE DATABASE command to create the shards, specifying the necessary parameters such as host, port, and database name.

Create Shard Map

The shard map is a table that maps the sharding key values to specific shards. Use the CREATE TABLE command to create the shard map table, specifying the necessary columns such as the sharding key and shard ID.

Insert Data into Shard Map

Use the INSERT INTO command to insert data into the shard map table, mapping each sharding key value to the appropriate shard ID.

Configure FWD

FWD is a middleware layer that handles routing requests to the appropriate shard based on the sharding key value. Configure FWD to handle requests to the adventureworks database, and to route those requests to the appropriate shard based on the shard map.

Migrate Data

Finally, migrate data from the original orders table to the appropriate shard, based on the shard map. This can be done using tools such as pg_dump and pg_restore, or using custom scripts.

With these steps, you can set up sharding with FWD for the adventureworks database in PostgreSQL, allowing you to scale out your database horizontally and improve performance.

Recipe#10: Configure Sharding with Citusdata

Configuring sharding with Citusdata in PostgreSQL involves using the Citus extension to partition data across multiple nodes, typically based on a specific key or range of keys. Here are the steps to configure sharding with Citusdata for the adventureworks database:

Install Citus Extension

Install the Citus extension on each node where you want to store data. This can be done using the CREATE EXTENSION command, or by installing the extension from source.

Choose Sharding Key

The sharding key is the column or set of columns used to partition the data across multiple nodes. For example, if you want to shard the orders table in the adventureworks database, you could use the customer_id column as the sharding key.

Create Distributed Table

Use the CREATE TABLE command with the DISTRIBUTED BY clause to create a distributed table, specifying the necessary columns such as the sharding key. For example:

```
CREATE TABLE orders (
  id SERIAL PRIMARY KEY,
  order_date DATE NOT NULL,
  customer_id INTEGER NOT NULL,
  ...
) DISTRIBUTED BY (customer_id);
```

This statement creates a orders table that is distributed across multiple nodes based on the customer_id column.

Migrate Data

Migrate data from the original orders table to the distributed table using tools such as pg_dump and pg_restore, or using custom scripts.

Optimize Performance

As with any database, there are several strategies to optimize performance, such as indexing, query optimization, and load balancing. Citus provides additional features such as distributed indexes and distributed SQL that can further optimize performance.

Add Nodes

To scale out your database horizontally, add additional nodes to the cluster using the citus_add_node command. This will automatically rebalance the data across all nodes, ensuring even distribution of data.

With these steps, you can configure sharding with Citusdata for the adventureworks database in PostgreSQL, allowing you to scale out your database horizontally and improve performance.

Recipe#11: Repair Shards

Repairing shards in a sharded PostgreSQL cluster involves fixing data inconsistencies or other issues that may arise due to hardware or software failures. Here are the steps to repair shards in a Citusdata sharded cluster for the adventureworks database:

Identify the Problem

Use monitoring tools and query logs to identify the nature of the problem with the shard. This may include data inconsistencies, network issues, hardware failures, or other problems.

Take the Shard Offline

If the problem is severe enough, take the shard offline to prevent further data inconsistencies or other issues. Use the DROP NODE command to remove the node from the cluster.

Repair the Problem

Depending on the nature of the problem, there may be several strategies to repair the shard. For example, if there are data inconsistencies, you may need to use data replication tools such as pg_dump and pg_restore to restore the data on the node. Alternatively, you may need to replace hardware or fix network issues to restore the node to proper operation.

Rejoin the Shard

Once the problem has been resolved, rejoin the shard to the cluster using the citus_add_node command. This will automatically rebalance the data across all nodes, ensuring even distribution of data.

Monitor and Optimize Performance

After repairing the shard, monitor the performance of the cluster to ensure that it is operating as expected. Use strategies such as indexing, query optimization, and load balancing to optimize performance as needed.

By following these steps, you can repair shards in a Citusdata sharded cluster for the adventureworks database, ensuring high availability and reliability for your data.

Chapter 7: Solving Replication, Scalability & High Availability

Recipe#1: Using Master-Slave Replication

Master-Slave Replication is a technique used to create a copy of the master database, called a slave or replica, to achieve high availability and scalability. This technique involves copying the data from the master database to one or more slave databases in real-time, using a process called streaming replication. This means that any changes made to the master database are immediately replicated to the slave databases, ensuring that all the databases are always in sync.

To use Master-Slave Replication to scale the given PostgreSQL database, we first need to set up a master database and one or more slave databases. Here are the steps:

Setup Master Database

Install PostgreSQL on the server where the master database will be hosted.

Create a new database using the following command: createdb dbname

Create a new user and grant it replication privileges using the following commands:

```
CREATE USER replication_user WITH REPLICATION PASSWORD
'password';
GRANT REPLICATION TO replication_user;
```

Modify the PostgreSQL configuration file, postgresql.conf, to allow replication by setting the following parameters:

```
wal_level = replica
max_wal_senders = 10
wal_keep_segments = 10
```

Restart the PostgreSQL service to apply the changes.

Setup Slave Database

Install PostgreSQL on the server where the slave database will be hosted.

Create a new database using the following command: createdb dbname

Modify the PostgreSQL configuration file, postgresql.conf, to allow replication by setting the following parameters:

```
hot_standby = on
```

Create a recovery.conf file in the data directory of the slave database and configure it with the following parameters:

```
standby_mode = 'on'
primary_conninfo = 'host=master_ip_address port=5432 user=replication_user password=password'
```

Replace master_ip_address, replication_user, and password with the actual values for your master database.

Start PostgreSQL Dervice on Slave Database

Connect to the master database and create a replication slot using the following command:

```
SELECT * FROM
pg_create_physical_replication_slot('replication_slot_name');
```

Note: Replace replication_slot_name with a unique name for your replication slot.

Verify that the replication slot has been created using the following command:

```
SELECT * FROM pg_replication_slots;
```

Connect to the slave database and start streaming replication by running the following command:

```
pg_basebackup -h master_ip_address -D /path/to/data/directory -P -U replication_user -R
```

Note: Replace master_ip_address, /path/to/data/directory, and replication_user with the actual values for your master database.

<u>Start PostgreSQL Service on Slave Database</u>

Once the replication is set up, any changes made to the master database will be immediately replicated to the slave database(s), allowing for high availability and scalability. To scale further, you can add more slave databases as needed.

Recipe#2: Setup Delay Standby

Setting up a Delayed Standby is a technique used to introduce a delay in the replication process between the master and slave databases. This technique can be useful in scenarios where you need to be able to recover from data corruption or human error.

Here are the steps to set up Delayed Standby in PostgreSQL:

Create a replication slot and a standby server as described in the previous solution.

Configure the standby server with the replication settings by modifying the postgresql.conf file as follows:

```
hot_standby = on
primary_conninfo = 'host=master_ip_address port=5432 user=replication_user password=password'
recovery_target_timeline = 'latest'
```

Note: Replace the master_ip_address, replication_user, and password with your actual values.

Create a recovery.conf file in the standby data directory, which tells PostgreSQL to use delayed replication.

```
standby_mode = on
primary_conninfo = 'host=master_ip_address port=5432 user=replication_user password=password'
recovery_target_timeline = 'latest'
recovery_target_time = 'YYYY-MM-DD HH:MI:SS'
```

Note: Replace the master_ip_address, replication_user, password, and YYYY-MM-DD

HH:MI:SS with your actual values. The recovery_target_time parameter is used to specify the delay in the replication process.

Start the standby server and verify that replication is working by checking the logs.

To test the delayed replication, you can perform a test on the master database and then use the pg_wal_replay_pause() function on the standby server to introduce a delay.

For example, to introduce a delay of 1 hour, run the following command on the standby server:

SELECT pg_wal_replay_pause(now() - interval '1 hour');

This will pause the replay of the WAL logs for 1 hour, after which it will resume automatically.

Note: Delayed Standby can introduce a delay in the replication process, which means that there will be a delay in the availability of the replicated data on the standby server. This technique should be used only when necessary and after careful consideration of the trade-offs involved.

Recipe#3: Install and Configure 'repmgr'

Repmgr is a popular tool used to manage replication and failover in PostgreSQL. It provides automated management and monitoring of PostgreSQL replication clusters, making it easier to set up and maintain PostgreSQL replication environments. Here are the steps to install and configure Repmgr in PostgreSQL 15:

Install Repmgr

Install the repmgr package on all the nodes in the replication cluster using the following command:

sudo apt-get install repmgr

Install the PostgreSQL client packages on all the nodes in the replication cluster using the following command:

sudo apt-get install postgresql-client

Configure Repmgr

Create a repmgr user on all the nodes in the replication cluster using the following command:

sudo -u postgres createuser repmgr --createrole --superuser --login

Create a repmgr database on all the nodes in the replication cluster using the following command:

sudo -u postgres createdb repmgr -O repmgr

Configure the repmgr configuration file (repmgr.conf) on the primary node with the following settings:

node_id = 1
node_name = primary
conninfo = host=primary_ip_address user=repmgr dbname=repmgr
data_directory = /path/to/postgresql/data

Note: Replace primary_ip_address and /path/to/postgresql/data with the actual values for your primary node.

Copy the repmgr.conf file to all the other nodes in the replication cluster.

Initialize the repmgr metadata on the primary node using the following command:

repmgr primary register

Note: This command will create the repmgr schema and tables in the repmgr database, and add the primary node to the metadata.

Check that the metadata is correct using the following command:

repmgr cluster show

Start Replication

Set up streaming replication between the primary node and the standby node(s) using the standard PostgreSQL streaming replication techniques as described in the previous solution.

On each standby node, register it with repmgr using the following command:

```
repmgr standby register
```

Check that the replication is working correctly using the following command:

```
repmgr cluster show
```

Note: This command will display the status of all the nodes in the replication cluster. Failover:

In the event of a primary node failure, promote a standby node to become the new primary node using the following command:

```
repmgr standby promote
```

This command will stop the old primary node, promote the designated standby node to become the new primary node, and update the repmgr metadata accordingly.

Repmgr provides many other features, including monitoring, automatic failover, and automatic reconfiguration of the replication cluster. These features can be configured by modifying the repmgr.conf file.

Recipe#4: Cloning Database with 'repmgr'

To clone a PostgreSQL database using repmgr, you can use the repmgr standby clone command. This command creates a new standby node by cloning an existing standby or primary node in the replication cluster.

Here are the steps to clone a PostgreSQL database using repmgr:

Choose the Source Node

Decide which node in the replication cluster you want to use as the source for the clone.

This can be either a primary node or a standby node.

Create a New Node

Create a new node for the clone by installing PostgreSQL and repmgr, and configuring the PostgreSQL and repmgr settings as you would for any other standby node.

Ensure that the new node has access to the same data directory as the source node.

Clone the Source Node

On the new node, use the repmgr standby clone command to clone the source node.

The basic syntax of the command is as follows:

```
repmgr standby clone SOURCE_NODE_CONNINFO
DEST_NODE_CONNINFO [options]
```

SOURCE_NODE_CONNINFO is the connection information for the source node.

DEST_NODE_CONNINFO is the connection information for the new node.

[options] are any additional options you want to specify, such as --dry-run to simulate the cloning process.

For example, to clone a standby node with the connection information host=source_ip_address user=repmgr dbname=repmgr port=5432 to a new node with the connection information host=new_ip_address user=repmgr dbname=repmgr port=5432, you would run the following command on the new node:

```
repmgr standby clone host=source_ip_address user=repmgr dbname=repmgr
port=5432 host=new_ip_address user=repmgr dbname=repmgr port=5432
```

Verify the Clone

After the cloning process completes, verify that the new node is functioning as a standby node by using the repmgr cluster show command on any node in the replication cluster. The new node should be listed as a standby node, and replication should be working correctly.

Note: The cloning process creates a new standby node, which is an exact replica of the source node at the time of the cloning. To keep the new node in sync with the source node, you should ensure that streaming replication is enabled and working correctly between the two nodes.

Recipe#5: Perform PITR Recovery using Delay Standby

Performing Point-in-Time Recovery (PITR) with a delayed standby node involves restoring the standby node to a specific point in time in the past, after introducing a delay in the replication process. Here are the steps to perform PITR recovery using a delayed standby node in PostgreSQL:

Determine Recovery Point

Identify the specific point in time to which you want to recover the database.

Note the timestamp of the recovery point.

Create recovery.conf File

Create a recovery.conf file in the data directory of the delayed standby node.
In the recovery.conf file, set the following parameters:

```
standby_mode = on
primary_conninfo = 'host=master_ip_address port=5432 user=replication_user
password=password'
recovery_target_timeline = 'latest'
recovery_target_time = 'YYYY-MM-DD HH:MI:SS'
```

master_ip_address, replication_user, and password should be replaced with the actual values for your master database.

YYYY-MM-DD HH:MI:SS should be replaced with the timestamp of the recovery point.

Save and close the recovery.conf file.

Start the Recovery Process

Stop the PostgreSQL service on the delayed standby node.

Copy the WAL archive files from the master database to the delayed standby node up to the recovery point.

Start the PostgreSQL service on the delayed standby node.

The recovery process should start automatically and continue until the database has been recovered to the specified point in time.

Verify the Recovery

Verify that the database has been recovered to the specified point in time by checking the contents of the database and comparing them to a known good state.

Ensure that the delay standby node is now fully operational and synchronized with the master database.

Note: Delayed standby nodes introduce a delay in the replication process, which means that the recovered database may be out of sync with the master database by a certain amount of time. This should be taken into consideration when performing PITR recovery using a delayed standby node. Additionally, ensure that you have sufficient disk space to store the WAL archive files needed for the recovery process.

Recipe#6: Deploy High Availability Cluster with Patroni

Patroni is an open-source tool that provides High Availability (HA) for PostgreSQL. It is a Python-based solution that simplifies the management and deployment of PostgreSQL HA clusters. Patroni uses the etcd key-value store to store and manage the configuration and state information for the PostgreSQL cluster, and it provides automatic failover and replication management for PostgreSQL.

Here are the steps to deploy a High Availability cluster with Patroni:

Install and Configure etcd

Install etcd on a separate server or node outside of the PostgreSQL cluster.

Configure etcd to listen on a specific IP address and port.

Ensure that etcd is accessible from all the nodes in the PostgreSQL cluster.

Install and Configure Patroni

Install Patroni on all the nodes in the PostgreSQL cluster.

Configure Patroni on each node with the appropriate settings, such as the connection information for the PostgreSQL instance, the location of the etcd server, and the cluster name.

Ensure that the etcd endpoints and cluster name are consistent across all the nodes in the cluster.

Initialize PostgreSQL Cluster

On the primary node, initialize the PostgreSQL cluster using the pg_ctl initdb command.

Create a PostgreSQL user and database for replication purposes, and grant replication privileges to the user.

Start the PostgreSQL instance on the primary node.

Start Patroni Instances

Start the Patroni instances on all the nodes in the cluster.

Patroni will automatically discover the primary node and the standby nodes, and configure replication between them.

Verify that replication is working correctly by checking the PostgreSQL logs.

Test the Failover

To test the failover, simulate a failure of the primary node by stopping the PostgreSQL service or shutting down the server.

Patroni will automatically detect the failure and promote one of the standby nodes to become the new primary node.

Verify that the new primary node is operational and that replication is working correctly.

Note: Patroni provides many additional features, such as automated backup and restore, monitoring, and logging. These features can be configured by modifying the Patroni configuration file (patroni.yml). Additionally, Patroni can be integrated with other tools and technologies, such as Kubernetes, to provide even greater flexibility and scalability.

Recipe#7: Using HAProxy and PgBouncer for High Availability

HAProxy and PgBouncer are two popular open-source tools used to provide High Availability for PostgreSQL databases. Here are the steps to use HAProxy and PgBouncer for high availability of a PostgreSQL database:

Install HAProxy and PgBouncer

Install HAProxy and PgBouncer on a separate server or node outside of the PostgreSQL cluster.

Configure HAProxy to listen on a specific IP address and port, and to forward traffic to the PgBouncer instances.

Configure PgBouncer with the appropriate settings, such as the connection information for the PostgreSQL instances and the pool mode.

Configure PostgreSQL Instances

Configure the PostgreSQL instances to allow connections from the HAProxy and PgBouncer servers.

Ensure that the PostgreSQL instances are configured with the appropriate settings, such as the maximum number of connections and the authentication method.

Start the PgBouncer Instances

Start the PgBouncer instances on all the nodes in the PostgreSQL cluster.

Configure the PgBouncer instances to use the same configuration file and to listen on the same IP address and port.

Start the HAProxy Server

Start the HAProxy server and configure it to balance traffic between the PgBouncer instances.

Ensure that the HAProxy configuration is set up with the appropriate settings, such as the load balancing algorithm and the health check method.

Test the Failover

To test the failover, simulate a failure of one of the PostgreSQL instances by stopping the PostgreSQL service or shutting down the server.

HAProxy will automatically detect the failure and redirect traffic to the remaining PostgreSQL instances.

PgBouncer will automatically reconnect to the remaining PostgreSQL instances and continue to balance the connection pool.

Note: HAProxy and PgBouncer provide many additional features, such as SSL support, connection pooling, and query routing. These features can be configured by modifying the HAProxy and PgBouncer configuration files. Additionally, HAProxy and PgBouncer can be integrated with other tools and technologies, such as Kubernetes, to provide even greater flexibility and scalability.

Recipe#8: Perform Database Upgrade on Replication Cluster

A replication cluster is a group of PostgreSQL database instances that are configured to replicate data between them. Replication clusters are used to provide High Availability (HA), load balancing, and disaster recovery capabilities for PostgreSQL databases. The replication cluster typically consists of a primary database instance and one or more standby database instances that are configured to replicate the data from the primary instance.

Performing a database upgrade on a replication cluster involves upgrading the primary database instance and then upgrading the standby database instances. Here are the steps to perform a database upgrade on a replication cluster:

Upgrade the Primary Database Instance

Stop the PostgreSQL service on the primary database instance.

Install the new version of PostgreSQL on the primary database instance.

Run the upgrade script to upgrade the data directory to the new version.

Modify the PostgreSQL configuration files as necessary for the new version.

Start the PostgreSQL service on the primary database instance.

Upgrade the Standby Database Instances

Stop the PostgreSQL service on each standby database instance.

Install the new version of PostgreSQL on each standby database instance.

Run the upgrade script to upgrade the data directory to the new version.

Modify the PostgreSQL configuration files as necessary for the new version.

Start the PostgreSQL service on each standby database instance.

Test the Replication

Verify that the replication is working correctly by checking the PostgreSQL logs and the replication status on each standby database instance.

Ensure that the standby database instances are fully synchronized with the primary database instance.

Note: It is important to ensure that all the instances in the replication cluster are running the same version of PostgreSQL to avoid compatibility issues and other problems. Additionally, it is recommended to perform a backup of the database before upgrading to ensure that you have a known good state in case of problems during the upgrade process.

CHAPTER 8: BLOB, JSON QUERY, CAST OPERATOR & CONNECTIONS

Recipe#1: Perform Querying

To query the given PostgreSQL database, you need to follow these steps:

Download the Dataset

First, download the data.zip file from the provided link (https://github.com/kittenpub/database-repository/blob/main/data.zip) and extract it to a folder on your local machine.

Create New PostgreSQL Database

Open the command prompt or terminal and run the following command to create a new database:

```
createdb adventureworks
```

Import the Extracted SQL File

Navigate to the folder where you extracted the data.zip file and locate the awbuild.sql file.

Import the SQL file into the adventureworks database using the following command:

```
psql -U username -d adventureworks -f awbuild.sql
```

Replace username with your PostgreSQL username. You may be prompted for a password, so provide the correct one for your PostgreSQL installation.

Connect to PostgreSQL Database

Use the following command to connect to the adventureworks database:

```
psql -U username -d adventureworks
```

Replace username with your PostgreSQL username.

Query the Database

Now you can run SQL queries on the adventureworks database. For example, to query all records from the product table, execute the following SQL command:

SELECT * FROM product;

Remember that you can replace this query with any other SQL query you want to run on the adventureworks database.

Exit PostgreSQL Prompt

To exit the PostgreSQL prompt, type \q and press Enter.

These steps should help you query the given PostgreSQL database using PostgreSQL 15. Confirm you have PostgreSQL 15 installed and configured on your machine before performing these steps.

Recipe#2: Import BLOB Data Types

To import BLOB data types (Binary Large Objects) into PostgreSQL, you'll need to use the bytea data type. The bytea data type is used to store binary data like images, audio files, or other binary files.

Following is an practical illustration of how to import BLOB data into a PostgreSQL table:

Create New Table with bytea Column

```
CREATE TABLE files (
  id SERIAL PRIMARY KEY,
  file_name VARCHAR(255),
  file_data bytea
);
```

This creates a table called files with an id, a file_name, and a file_data column to store the BLOB data.

Convert Bbinary File to Hex-encoded String

Before you import the binary file into PostgreSQL, you need to convert it into a hex-encoded string. You can use Python to achieve this. Following is a simple Python script that reads a file and outputs its hex-encoded string representation:

```python
def convert_to_hex(file_path):
    with open(file_path, 'rb') as file:
        return '\\x' + file.read().hex()


file_path = 'path/to/your/file.ext'
hex_string = convert_to_hex(file_path)
print(hex_string)
```

Replace 'path/to/your/file.ext' with the path to your binary file. Run the script and note the output hex-encoded string.

Import BLOB Data into Table

Now, you can insert the hex-encoded string into the files table. Use the following SQL query to insert the data:

```sql
INSERT INTO files (file_name, file_data)
VALUES ('your_file_name.ext', E'\\xYOUR_HEX_STRING');
```

Replace 'your_file_name.ext' with the name of your binary file, and \\xYOUR_HEX_STRING with the hex-encoded string you got from the Python script (including the \\x prefix).

Retrieve BLOB Data

To retrieve the BLOB data from the table, you can use a SELECT query like this:

```sql
SELECT file_name, file_data FROM files WHERE id = 1;
```

This will return the file_name and file_data for the record with id 1. To work with the BLOB data in your application, you might need to convert it back to its original binary form.

These steps demonstrate how to import BLOB data types into a PostgreSQL table using the bytea data type.

Recipe#3: Running Queries using Shell Script

To run queries using a shell script in PostgreSQL 15, you can create a shell script that connects to the database and executes SQL commands using the psql command-line tool.

The given below is an example of a shell script that runs a query on a PostgreSQL database:

Create a new file with the .sh extension, e.g., query_example.sh.

Add the following content to the file:

```bash
#!/bin/bash

# Replace these variables with your own PostgreSQL credentials
DB_NAME="your_database_name"
DB_USER="your_postgresql_username"
DB_PASS="your_postgresql_password"
DB_HOST="localhost"
DB_PORT="5432"

# SQL query to execute
QUERY="SELECT * FROM your_table_name;"

# Execute the SQL query using psql
export PGPASSWORD="$DB_PASS"
psql -h "$DB_HOST" -p "$DB_PORT" -U "$DB_USER" -d "$DB_NAME" -c "$QUERY"
unset PGPASSWORD
```

Replace the placeholders with the appropriate values for your PostgreSQL setup: your_database_name, your_postgresql_username, your_postgresql_password, your_table_name, and any other connection details if needed (e.g., DB_HOST and DB_PORT).

Save the shell script file and make it executable:

```
chmod +x query_example.sh
```

Run the shell script:

```
./query_example.sh
```

This script will connect to the specified PostgreSQL database and execute the given SQL query.

The query result will be displayed in the terminal.

You can modify the QUERY variable in the shell script to execute different SQL queries, or you can add more queries by creating new variables and appending additional psql commands. Confirm to keep the single quotes and semicolon around the query.

Recipe#4: Working with Postgres JSON Query

PostgreSQL provides powerful support for working with JSON data using JSON and JSONB data types. In the adventureworks database, there is no JSON data by default. However, I will provide you with an example of how to work with JSON data in a PostgreSQL table, which you can apply to the adventureworks database or any other PostgreSQL database.

Create Table with JSONB Column

```
CREATE TABLE customer_info (
 id SERIAL PRIMARY KEY,
 data JSONB
);
```

This creates a table called customer_info with an id column and a data column to store JSON data.

Insert JSON Data into Table

```
INSERT INTO customer_info (data) VALUES
('{"name": "John Doe", "email": "john@example.com", "age": 30, "address":
{"street": "123 Main St", "city": "New York", "state": "NY", "zip":
"10001"}}'),
('{"name": "Jane Doe", "email": "jane@example.com", "age": 28, "address":
{"street": "456 Main St", "city": "New York", "state": "NY", "zip":
"10002"}}');
```

This inserts two records with JSON data into the customer_info table.

Query JSON

You can query JSON data using various PostgreSQL JSON functions and operators. Here are some examples:

Select a specific JSON field

```
SELECT data->>'name' AS name FROM customer_info;
```

This query extracts the 'name' field from the JSON data and returns it as a column named 'name'.

Filter rows based on a JSON field

```
SELECT * FROM customer_info WHERE data->>'age'::integer >= 30;
```

This query returns all records where the 'age' field in the JSON data is greater than or equal to 30.

Update a JSON field

```
UPDATE customer_info SET data = jsonb_set(data, '{address,zip}', '"10003"')
WHERE data->>'email' = 'john@example.com';
```

This query updates the 'zip' field inside the 'address' object for the record with the email 'john@example.com'.

Check if a JSON field exists

```
SELECT * FROM customer_info WHERE data ? 'email';
```

This query returns all records that have an 'email' field in their JSON data.

These examples should give you an idea of how to work with JSON data in PostgreSQL. You can apply these concepts to the adventureworks database or any other PostgreSQL database that contains JSON

Recipe#5: Working with Postgres CAST Operator

The PostgreSQL CAST operator is used to convert a value of one data type to another data type. You can use the CAST operator in various situations, such as converting data types in a query, transforming data when inserting or updating records, and filtering data based on a specific data type.

Here are some examples of how to use the CAST operator in PostgreSQL:

Converting Data Types in SELECT Query

```
SELECT CAST(some_column AS integer) FROM some_table;
```

This query converts the values in some_column to the integer data type.

Alternatively, you can use the :: syntax for casting:

```
SELECT some_column::integer FROM some_table;
```

Converting Data Types When Inserting Records

Suppose you have a table called prices with the following structure:

```sql
CREATE TABLE prices (
  id SERIAL PRIMARY KEY,
  price NUMERIC(10, 2)
);
```

If you want to insert a new record with a price value as a string, you can use the CAST operator:

```sql
INSERT INTO prices (price) VALUES (CAST('10.50' AS NUMERIC(10, 2)));
```

Or using the :: syntax:

```sql
INSERT INTO prices (price) VALUES ('10.50'::NUMERIC(10, 2));
```

Converting Data Types When Updating Records

Suppose you want to update the price value of a specific record and the new price value is a string:

```sql
UPDATE prices SET price = CAST('15.75' AS NUMERIC(10, 2)) WHERE id = 1;
```

Or using the :: syntax:

```sql
UPDATE prices SET price = '15.75'::NUMERIC(10, 2) WHERE id = 1;
```

Filtering Data Based on Specific Data Type

Suppose you have a table called orders with a created_at column of type timestamp and you want to fetch records created on a specific date:

```sql
SELECT * FROM orders WHERE CAST(created_at AS date) = '2022-10-01';
```

Or using the :: syntax:

```sql
SELECT * FROM orders WHERE created_at::date = '2022-10-01';
```

These examples demonstrate how to use the PostgreSQL CAST operator to convert values between different data types. You can apply these concepts to any PostgreSQL database, including the adventureworks database.

Recipe#6: Assuring Database Consistency and Integrity

To confirm the database consistency and integrity in PostgreSQL 15, you can use several built-in mechanisms such as Constraints, Triggers, Foreign Keys, and Views.

Here are some practical examples of how to confirm database consistency and integrity in PostgreSQL 15:

Constraints

Constraints are rules that restrict the values in a column or set of columns. You can use constraints to ensure that the data in your table meets specific criteria.
For example, to ensure that the email column in the customer table is unique and not null, you can create a unique constraint and a not-null constraint:

```sql
ALTER TABLE customer ADD CONSTRAINT unique_email UNIQUE
(email);
ALTER TABLE customer ALTER COLUMN email SET NOT NULL;
```

This constraint ensures that each customer has a unique and non-null email address.

Triggers

Triggers are special types of functions that automatically execute when certain events occur, such as an insert, update, or delete operation on a table. You can use triggers to perform custom validation and maintain referential integrity.

For example, to prevent an order from being deleted if it has related items in the order_item table, you can create a trigger:

```sql
CREATE OR REPLACE FUNCTION delete_order() RETURNS TRIGGER
```

```
AS $$
BEGIN
 IF EXISTS (SELECT 1 FROM order_item WHERE order_id = OLD.id)
THEN
   RAISE EXCEPTION 'Cannot delete order with related items';
 END IF;
 RETURN OLD;
END;
$$ LANGUAGE plpgsql;


CREATE TRIGGER delete_order_trigger BEFORE DELETE ON orders
FOR EACH ROW EXECUTE FUNCTION delete_order();
```

This trigger ensures that you cannot delete an order if it has any related items.

Foreign Keys

Foreign keys are constraints that enforce referential integrity between two tables. You can use foreign keys to ensure that data in one table corresponds to data in another table.

For example, to create a foreign key constraint between the order_item and product tables, you can use the following command:

```
ALTER TABLE order_item ADD CONSTRAINT fk_product FOREIGN KEY
(product_id) REFERENCES product(id);
```

This foreign key constraint ensures that each product ID in the order_item table corresponds to a valid ID in the product table.

Views

Views are virtual tables that are based on the result of a SELECT query. You can use views to simplify complex queries and ensure consistent data representation.

For example, to create a view that shows the total sales for each product, you can use the following command:

```sql
CREATE VIEW product_sales AS
SELECT product_id, SUM(quantity * price) AS total_sales
FROM order_item
GROUP BY product_id;
```

This view ensures that you always get accurate total sales data for each product.

These are some practical examples of how to confirm database consistency and integrity in PostgreSQL 15 using built-in mechanisms such as Constraints, Triggers, Foreign Keys, and Views. By applying these techniques, you can ensure that your data is accurate, reliable, and consistent.

CHAPTER 9: AUTHENTICATION, AUDIT & ENCRYPTION

Recipe#1: Manage Roles, Membership, Attributes, Authentication and Authorizations

PostgreSQL provides a robust and flexible security model that allows for fine-grained control over roles, authentication, authorization, and attributes. Here are the steps to manage roles membership, attributes, authentication, and authorizations in PostgreSQL:

Creating Roles

In PostgreSQL, roles are used to represent users, groups, or applications. To create a role, use the CREATE ROLE statement. For example, to create a role called "sales", use the following statement:

```
CREATE ROLE sales;
```

Adding Members to Roles

Once you have created a role, you can add members to it using the GRANT statement. For example, to add a user called "alice" to the "sales" role, use the following statement:

```
GRANT sales TO alice;
```

Setting Role Attributes

PostgreSQL allows you to set various attributes for a role, such as password, login, and valid until. To set attributes for a role, use the ALTER ROLE statement. For example, to set a password for the "sales" role, use the following statement:

```
ALTER ROLE sales PASSWORD 'password';
```

Authenticating Users

PostgreSQL provides several authentication methods, including password, ident, and LDAP. The authentication method is specified in the pg_hba.conf file. To use password authentication, set the authentication method to "md5" and add a password for the user. For example, to set a password for the "alice" user, use the following statement:

ALTER USER alice PASSWORD 'password';

Setting User Authorizations

Once you have authenticated a user, you can set their authorizations using the GRANT statement. For example, to grant the "sales" role to the "alice" user, use the following statement:

GRANT sales TO alice;

Restricting User Access

You can also restrict user access using the REVOKE statement. For example, to revoke the "sales" role from the "alice" user, use the following statement:

REVOKE sales FROM alice;

Managing Object Permissions

In PostgreSQL, you can manage object permissions using the GRANT and REVOKE statements. For example, to grant SELECT permission on a table called "employees" to the "sales" role, use the following statement:

GRANT SELECT ON employees TO sales;

To revoke SELECT permission on the same table from the "sales" role, use the following statement:

REVOKE SELECT ON employees FROM sales;

By following these steps, you can effectively manage roles membership, attributes, authentication, and authorizations in PostgreSQL.

Recipe#2: Setting Up SSL Authentication

Setting up SSL authentication in PostgreSQL involves the following steps:

Generate SSL Certificate and Key Pair

You can either generate a self-signed SSL certificate and key pair or obtain a trusted SSL certificate from a trusted certificate authority (CA).

Configure PostgreSQL to use SSL

You can configure PostgreSQL to use SSL by adding the appropriate settings to the postgresql.conf file. The settings include ssl = on, ssl_cert_file, ssl_key_file, and ssl_ca_file.

For example, to enable SSL, set ssl = on in the postgresql.conf file. Then, specify the path to the SSL certificate and key files using the ssl_cert_file and ssl_key_file settings, respectively. If you are using a self-signed SSL certificate, you can skip the ssl_ca_file setting. If you are using a trusted SSL certificate, you need to specify the path to the CA certificate file using the ssl_ca_file setting.

Configure Client Authentication

To enable SSL authentication for clients, you need to specify the appropriate settings in the pg_hba.conf file. The settings include hostssl, cert, and clientcert.

For example, to require SSL authentication for a user called "alice" connecting from a specific IP address, add the following entry to the pg_hba.conf file:

```
hostssl all alice 192.168.1.100/24 cert clientcert=1
```

This entry specifies that SSL authentication is required for the user "alice" connecting from the IP address range 192.168.1.100/24. The clientcert=1 option indicates that the client must present a valid SSL certificate for authentication.

Test SSL Authentication

Once you have configured SSL authentication, you can test it by connecting to PostgreSQL using an SSL-enabled client, such as psql with the -sslmode=require option.

For example, to connect to PostgreSQL using psql with SSL authentication, use the following command:

```
psql "postgresql://alice@192.168.1.100/mydb?sslmode=require"
```

This command specifies that SSL authentication is required for the connection, and the client must present a valid SSL certificate for authentication.

By following these steps, you can set up SSL authentication in PostgreSQL to secure client connections to the database server.

Recipe#3: Configure Encryption

To configure encryption in PostgreSQL, you can use the Transparent Data Encryption (TDE) feature provided by various third-party tools or encrypt data at the application layer before storing it in the database. Here are the steps to configure TDE using one of the popular tools, OpenSSL:

Install OpenSSL

If OpenSSL is not already installed on your system, install it using the appropriate package manager for your operating system.

Generate Encryption Key

Use the OpenSSL command-line tool to generate an encryption key. For example, to generate a 256-bit AES encryption key, use the following command:

```
openssl rand -out mykey.bin 32
```

This command generates a random 256-bit key and saves it to a file called mykey.bin.

Encrypt Database Files

Use the OpenSSL command-line tool to encrypt the database files. For example, to encrypt a database called "mydb" located in the /var/lib/postgresql/data directory, use the following command:

```
openssl enc -aes-256-cbc -in /var/lib/postgresql/data/mydb -out
/var/lib/postgresql/data/mydb.enc -pass file:mykey.bin
```

This command encrypts the "mydb" database file using 256-bit AES encryption and saves the encrypted file to mydb.enc. The -pass file:mykey.bin option specifies that the encryption key is stored in the mykey.bin file.

<u>Modify PostgreSQL Configuration</u>

Modify the postgresql.conf file to specify the location of the encrypted database files. Add the following line to the file:

```
data_directory = '/var/lib/postgresql/data_encrypted'
```

This line specifies that the encrypted database files are located in the /var/lib/postgresql/data_encrypted directory.

<u>Start PostgreSQL</u>

Start the PostgreSQL server and verify that it is using the encrypted database files by connecting to it and running queries.

By following these steps, you can configure encryption in PostgreSQL using the OpenSSL tool to secure the database files. Note that this is just one way to configure encryption, and there are many other tools and methods available to encrypt data in PostgreSQL.

Recipe#4: Install and Configure pgAudit

pgAudit is a PostgreSQL extension that provides detailed audit logging capabilities for PostgreSQL database servers. It allows database administrators to log and monitor all SQL statements executed on the database server, including the user who executed the statement, the time it was executed, and the database object affected by the statement. This information can be used for security and compliance purposes, such as detecting unauthorized access, identifying performance bottlenecks, and tracking changes to sensitive data.

To install and configure pgAudit for your PostgreSQL database, follow these steps:

<u>Install pgAudit</u>

pgAudit can be installed using the PostgreSQL package manager, such as yum or apt-get, or by compiling from source code. To install pgAudit using the package manager, use the following command:

```
sudo apt-get install postgresql-14-pgaudit
```

Enable pgAudit

To enable pgAudit, add the pgAudit extension to the PostgreSQL server using the CREATE EXTENSION statement. For example, to enable pgAudit for a database called "mydb", use the following command:

```
psql -d mydb -c 'CREATE EXTENSION pgaudit;'
```

Configure pgAudit

pgAudit can be configured using the pgaudit.conf file, which is located in the PostgreSQL data directory. The file specifies which events should be logged, such as read or write statements, and which fields should be included in the log entries, such as the user name, database name, and statement text. The configuration can be customized to meet specific audit requirements.

For example, to log all read and write statements for the "mytable" table in the "mydb" database, add the following line to the pgaudit.conf file:

```
log = 'read, write' mydb.mytable
```

Restart PostgreSQL

After configuring pgAudit, restart the PostgreSQL server to apply the changes. Use the appropriate command for your operating system to restart the server. For example, on Ubuntu, use the following command:

```
sudo systemctl restart postgresql
```

Test pgAudit

To test pgAudit, execute some SQL statements on the database and verify that they are logged in the pgAudit log file. The log file is located in the PostgreSQL data directory and can be viewed using a text editor or the pgaudit_logfile view.

For example, to view the pgAudit log file for a database called "mydb", use the following command:

```
psql -d mydb -c 'SELECT * FROM pgaudit_log;'
```

By following these steps, you can install and configure pgAudit for your PostgreSQL database to provide detailed audit logging capabilities. Note that pgAudit is just one way to enable audit logging in PostgreSQL, and there are many other tools and methods available to audit PostgreSQL databases.

Recipe#5: Using Audit Log with PostgreSQL Trigger

Let us see below a practical example of using audit log with PostgreSQL trigger:

Consider that we have a table called "customers" with the following columns: id, name, email, and status. We want to log all changes to this table in an audit log table called "customers_audit". We can achieve this by creating a trigger on the "customers" table that inserts a row into the "customers_audit" table whenever a change is made to the "customers" table.

Create Audit Log Table

We need to create the "customers_audit" table with the columns that we want to log. For example:

```
CREATE TABLE customers_audit (
  id SERIAL PRIMARY KEY,
  timestamp TIMESTAMP DEFAULT NOW(),
  user_id INTEGER,
  action TEXT,
  old_data JSONB,
  new_data JSONB
);
```

Create Trigger Function

We need to create a trigger function that will be called whenever a change is made to the "customers" table. This function will insert a row into the "customers_audit" table with the old and new values of the changed row.

```
CREATE OR REPLACE FUNCTION customers_audit_trigger() RETURNS
```

```sql
TRIGGER AS $$
DECLARE
 data_old JSONB;
 data_new JSONB;
BEGIN
 IF TG_OP = 'DELETE' THEN
   data_old = row_to_json(OLD);
   INSERT INTO customers_audit (user_id, action, old_data)
   VALUES (current_user, TG_OP, data_old);
   RETURN OLD;
 ELSIF TG_OP = 'UPDATE' THEN
   data_old = row_to_json(OLD);
   data_new = row_to_json(NEW);
   INSERT INTO customers_audit (user_id, action, old_data, new_data)
   VALUES (current_user, TG_OP, data_old, data_new);
   RETURN NEW;
 ELSIF TG_OP = 'INSERT' THEN
   data_new = row_to_json(NEW);
   INSERT INTO customers_audit (user_id, action, new_data)
   VALUES (current_user, TG_OP, data_new);
   RETURN NEW;
 END IF;
 RETURN NULL;
END;
$$
LANGUAGE plpgsql;
```

Create the trigger: We need to create a trigger on the "customers" table that will call the "customers_audit_trigger" function whenever a change is made to the table.

```sql
CREATE TRIGGER customers_audit
AFTER INSERT OR UPDATE OR DELETE ON customers
```

FOR EACH ROW
EXECUTE FUNCTION customers_audit_trigger();

Now, whenever a change is made to the "customers" table, the trigger will call the "customers_audit_trigger" function, which will insert a row into the "customers_audit" table with the old and new values of the changed row, as well as the user who made the change and the type of change (insert, update, or delete).

To view the audit log, simply query the "customers_audit" table. For example, to view all changes made by a specific user:

SELECT * FROM customers_audit WHERE user_id = 123;

By using triggers in this way, we can easily log changes to any table in a PostgreSQL database and maintain a detailed audit trail.

Recipe#6: Using log_statement/Audit Trail

In PostgreSQL 15, the log_statement configuration parameter controls which SQL statements are logged to the server log. By default, log_statement is set to none, which means that no statements are logged.

Using log_statement

However, you can set it to one of the following values to log SQL statements:
- ddl: Log all data definition language (DDL) statements, such as CREATE, ALTER, and DROP.
- mod: Log all DDL and data modification language (DML) statements, such as INSERT, UPDATE, and DELETE.
- all: Log all statements, including DDL, DML, and utility statements, such as VACUUM and EXPLAIN.

To enable log_statement, you need to modify the postgresql.conf file and set the log_statement parameter to the desired value. For example, to log all statements, add the following line to the postgresql.conf file:

log_statement = 'all'

Once you have enabled log_statement, you can view the logged statements in the server log, which is usually located in the PostgreSQL data directory. You can also configure PostgreSQL to log statements to a separate file or send them to a remote log server.

The given below is a practical example of using log_statement to audit SQL statements in a PostgreSQL database:

Consider that we have a database called "sales" and we want to log all SQL statements executed on the database for security and compliance purposes. We can enable log_statement to log all statements to the server log, as follows:

Modify postgresql.conf File

Locate the postgresql.conf file in the PostgreSQL data directory and open it in a text editor. Add the following line to enable log_statement:

```
log_statement = 'all'
```

Restart PostgreSQL

Restart the PostgreSQL server to apply the changes. Use the appropriate command for your operating system to restart the server. For example, on Ubuntu, use the following command:

```
sudo systemctl restart postgresql
```

Execute SQL Statements

Execute some SQL statements on the "sales" database to generate some log entries. For example:

```
SELECT * FROM customers;
INSERT INTO orders (customer_id, total) VALUES (123, 100.00);
UPDATE customers SET name = 'Alice' WHERE id = 123;
```

View the Log

Open the server log file, which is usually located in the PostgreSQL data directory, and search for the logged statements. The logged statements will include the user who executed the statement, the time it was executed, and the statement text.

By using log_statement in this way, we can easily log SQL statements executed on a PostgreSQL database and maintain a detailed audit trail. Note that log_statement can generate a lot of log entries and can impact server performance, so it's important to use it judiciously and consider the performance implications.

Recipe#7: Install and Configure LDAP Authentication

LDAP (Lightweight Directory Access Protocol) authentication is a way of authenticating users against a centralized directory service, such as Microsoft Active Directory or OpenLDAP. With LDAP authentication, users can log in to a PostgreSQL database using their credentials stored in the directory service, rather than having to create a separate account in the database. This provides a centralized and secure way of managing user accounts across multiple applications and services.

To use LDAP authentication with PostgreSQL, you need to configure the pg_hba.conf file to use the LDAP authentication method. Here are the steps to configure LDAP authentication in PostgreSQL:

Install LDAP Authentication Package

You need to install the LDAP authentication package for PostgreSQL. The package is usually provided by your Linux distribution, such as openldap or ldap-utils.

Configure LDAP Client

You need to configure the LDAP client on the PostgreSQL server to connect to the LDAP directory service. The configuration includes the LDAP server name, port number, and search base.

Configure pg_hba.conf

You need to modify the pg_hba.conf file to specify the LDAP authentication method for the users you want to authenticate using LDAP. For example:

```
host    all         all         192.168.1.0/24        ldap
ldapserver=ldap.example.com ldapport=389 ldapprefix="cn="
```

```
ldapsuffix=",ou=users,dc=example,dc=com"
```

This line specifies that all users connecting from the IP address range 192.168.1.0/24 should be authenticated using LDAP against the server ldap.example.com on port 389. The ldapprefix and ldapsuffix options specify the format of the user's distinguished name (DN) in the LDAP directory.

Test LDAP Authentication

To test LDAP authentication, connect to the PostgreSQL database using a user account stored in the LDAP directory service. For example, use the following command:

```
psql -h localhost -U cn=john,ou=users,dc=example,dc=com -d mydb
```

This command connects to the "mydb" database using the user account with the DN cn=john,ou=users,dc=example,dc=com in the LDAP directory.

By following these steps, you can configure LDAP authentication in PostgreSQL to authenticate users against a centralized directory service. Note that LDAP authentication can provide a convenient and secure way of managing user accounts, but it requires some setup and configuration.

CHAPTER 10: IMPLEMENTING DATABASE BACKUP STRATEGIES

Recipe#1: Automate Database Backup

Let us see below how to automate the backup of the PostgreSQL AdventureWorks database:

Create Backup Script

Create a backup script that uses the pg_dump utility to backup the AdventureWorks database. For example:

```
#!/bin/bash
DATE=$(date +%Y-%m-%d_%H-%M-%S)
BACKUP_DIR=/path/to/backup/dir
DB_NAME=AdventureWorks
PG_DUMP=/usr/bin/pg_dump


$PG_DUMP -Fc $DB_NAME > $BACKUP_DIR/$DB_NAME-$DATE.dump
```

This script creates a backup file in the specified directory with the name "AdventureWorks-YYYY-MM-DD_HH-MM-SS.dump", where the date and time are the current date and time.

Make Backup Script Executable

Make the backup script executable using the following command:

```
chmod +x /path/to/backup/script.sh
```

Test the Backup Script

Test the backup script by running it manually and verifying that it creates a backup file in the specified directory.

Schedule the Backup

Use a cron job to schedule the backup script to run at regular intervals. For example, to run the backup script every day at midnight, add the following line to the crontab file:

0 0 * * * /path/to/backup/script.sh

This will run the backup script every day at midnight and create a new backup file with the current date and time.

By following these steps, you can automate the backup of the PostgreSQL AdventureWorks database and ensure that you have a regular backup in case of data loss or system failure. Note that it's important to store the backup files in a secure location and test the backup and restore process regularly to ensure that it's working correctly.

Recipe#2: Execute Continuous Archiving PostgreSQL Backup

Continuous Archiving PostgreSQL Backup is a technique that involves continuously archiving the transaction logs of a PostgreSQL database to a backup location. This allows for point-in-time recovery of the database in case of a failure.

Check out below how to set up continuous archiving backup for the AdventureWorks database:

Enable Archiving

In the postgresql.conf file, set the archive_mode parameter to on to enable archiving. For example:

archive_mode = on

This will enable the archive command to be executed for each transaction that is committed.

Setup the Archive Command

In the postgresql.conf file, set the archive_command parameter to specify the command to be executed for each transaction that is archived. For example:

archive_command = 'cp %p /path/to/backup/archive/%f'

This will copy each archived transaction log to the specified backup archive directory.

Create Base Backup

Create a base backup of the AdventureWorks database using the pg_basebackup utility. For example:

```
pg_basebackup -U postgres -D /path/to/backup/base -Ft -Xs -P
```

This will create a backup of the database cluster in the specified directory.

Start PostgreSQL with the backup as the data directory: Start PostgreSQL using the backup directory as the data directory. For example:

```
postgres -D /path/to/backup/base
```

Test the Archiving

Execute some transactions on the database and verify that the transaction logs are being archived to the backup archive directory.

By following these steps, you can set up continuous archiving backup for the AdventureWorks database and ensure that you have a continuous backup of the transaction logs for point-in-time recovery in case of a failure. Note that it's important to monitor the backup process and verify that the backup files are being created correctly.

Recipe#3: Working with 'pg_probackup' and 'pgBackRest'

pg_probackup and pgBackRest are popular backup and restore tools for PostgreSQL. Checkout below how to work with each tool:

pg_probackup

pg_probackup is a backup and recovery tool for PostgreSQL that provides features such as incremental backups, validation, and point-in-time recovery. Checkout below how to use pg_probackup:

Install pg_probackup

Install pg_probackup using the package manager of your operating system or by building from source.

Configure pg_probackup

Configure pg_probackup by creating a configuration file, which is usually located in the PostgreSQL data directory. The configuration file specifies options such as the backup directory, compression settings, and retention policy.

Create Backup

Create a backup using the pg_probackup backup command. For example:

```
pg_probackup backup -B /path/to/backup/dir -D /path/to/postgresql/data
```

This will create a full backup in the specified backup directory.

Validate the Backup

Validate the backup using the pg_probackup validate command. For example:

```
pg_probackup validate -B /path/to/backup/dir
```

This will verify the integrity of the backup and report any errors.

Restore the \Bbackup

Restore the backup using the pg_probackup restore command. For example:

```
pg_probackup restore -B /path/to/backup/dir -D /path/to/new/data/dir -i backup_id
```

This will restore the specified backup to the new data directory.

pgBackRest

pgBackRest is a backup and restore tool for PostgreSQL that provides features such as compression, incremental backups, and parallelism. Checkout below how to use pgBackRest:

Install pgBackRest

Install pgBackRest using the package manager of your operating system or by building from source.

Configure pgBackRest

Configure pgBackRest by creating a configuration file, which is usually located in the PostgreSQL data directory. The configuration file specifies options such as the backup directory, compression settings, and retention policy.

Create Backup

Create a backup using the pgbackrest backup command. For example:

```
pgbackrest backup --pg1-path=/path/to/postgresql/data --backup-path=/path/to/backup/dir
```

This will create a full backup in the specified backup directory.

Validate the Backup

Validate the backup using the pgbackrest check command. For example:

```
pgbackrest check --stanza=default
```

This will verify the integrity of the backup and report any errors.

Restore the Backup

Restore the backup using the pgbackrest restore command. For example:

```
pgbackrest restore --pg1-path=/path/to/new/data/dir --backup-path=/path/to/backup/dir --type=full
```

This will restore the specified backup to the new data directory.

By using pg_probackup or pgBackRest, you can create reliable and efficient backups of your PostgreSQL database and ensure that you have a solid backup and recovery strategy.

Note that both tools have extensive documentation and support for advanced features, so it's important to read the documentation carefully and test the backup and restore process thoroughly.

Recipe#4: Install and Configure Barman

Barman is an open-source backup and recovery tool for PostgreSQL that is designed for enterprise environments. Barman provides features such as remote backups, incremental backups, retention policies, and point-in-time recovery. Checkout below how to install and configure Barman:

Install Barman

Install Barman using the package manager of your operating system or by building from source.

Configure Barman

Configure Barman by creating a configuration file, which is usually located in the Barman data directory. The configuration file specifies options such as the backup directory, compression settings, and retention policy. Below is an example configuration file:

```
[barman]
barman_home = /var/lib/barman
log_file = /var/log/barman/barman.log
minimum_redundancy = 1

[pg]
description = PostgreSQL
conninfo = host=pgserver user=barman dbname=postgres
backup_method = rsync
retention_policy = REDUNDANCY 1
```

This configuration file specifies that the backup directory is located in the Barman home directory, the backup method is rsync, and the retention policy is to keep at least one full backup.

Add Barman User to PostgreSQL

Add the Barman user to PostgreSQL with the necessary privileges to perform backups. For example:

CREATE USER barman WITH SUPERUSER LOGIN;

Create Backup

Create a backup using the barman backup command. For example:

barman backup pg

This will create a full backup of the PostgreSQL database specified in the configuration file.

Verify the Backup

Verify the backup using the barman check command. For example:

barman check pg

This will verify the integrity of the backup and report any errors.

Restore the Backup

Restore the backup using the barman recover command. For example:

barman recover pg latest /path/to/new/data/dir

This will restore the most recent backup to the new data directory.

By using Barman, you can create a reliable and efficient backup and recovery strategy for your PostgreSQL database in an enterprise environment. Note that Barman has extensive documentation and support for advanced features, so it's important to read the documentation carefully and test the backup and restore process thoroughly.

Recipe#5: Perform Incremental/Differential Backup

Performing incremental or differential backups in PostgreSQL 15 involves creating backups that only contain changes made to the database since the last full backup. This can be useful for reducing backup times and storage requirements. Below is how to perform incremental and differential backups in PostgreSQL 15:

Incremental Backup

Create a full backup

Create a full backup of the PostgreSQL database using a backup tool such as pg_dump, pg_dumpall, pg_basebackup, or a third-party tool such as pgBackRest or Barman. For example:

```
pg_dumpall -U postgres -f /path/to/full/backup.sql
```

Create incremental backup

Create an incremental backup of the PostgreSQL database using a tool that supports incremental backups, such as pgBackRest or Barman. For example, to create an incremental backup with pgBackRest:

```
pgbackrest backup --type=incremental --pg1-path=/path/to/postgresql/data --backup-path=/path/to/incremental/backup
```

This will create an incremental backup that contains changes made to the database since the last full backup.

Restore the backup

To restore the database, you need to first restore the full backup and then apply the incremental backup. For example, to restore the backup using pgBackRest:

```
pgbackrest restore --type=incremental --pg1-path=/path/to/new/data/dir --backup-path=/path/to/full/backup --delta /path/to/incremental/backup
```

This will restore the full backup to the new data directory and then apply the changes in the incremental backup.

Differential Backup

Create a full backup
Create a full backup of the PostgreSQL database using a backup tool such as pg_dump, pg_dumpall, pg_basebackup, or a third-party tool such as pgBackRest or Barman. For example:

```
pg_dumpall -U postgres -f /path/to/full/backup.sql
```

Create a differential backup
Create a differential backup of the PostgreSQL database using a tool that supports differential backups, such as pgBackRest or Barman. For example, to create a differential backup with pgBackRest:

```
pgbackrest backup --type=diff --pg1-path=/path/to/postgresql/data --backup-path=/path/to/differential/backup
```

This will create a differential backup that contains changes made to the database since the last full backup.

Restore the backup
To restore the database, you need to first restore the full backup and then apply the differential backup. For example, to restore the backup using pgBackRest:

```
pgbackrest restore --type=diff --pg1-path=/path/to/new/data/dir --backup-path=/path/to/full/backup --delta /path/to/differential/backup
```

This will restore the full backup to the new data directory and then apply the changes in the differential backup.

By using incremental or differential backups, you can reduce the backup times and storage requirements of your PostgreSQL database and ensure that you have a reliable backup and recovery strategy in case of a failure. Note that it's important to test the backup and restore process thoroughly to ensure that it's working correctly.

Recipe#6: Execute Schema Level Backup

A schema-level backup in PostgreSQL involves backing up a specific schema or set of schemas in a database. This can be useful for selectively backing up parts of a database, such as a particular application or module. Below is how to execute a schema-level backup for the AdventureWorks database:

Create Backup Directory

Create a backup directory where the schema-level backup files will be stored. For example:

```
mkdir /path/to/schema/backup
```

Create Schema-level Backup

Create a schema-level backup using the pg_dump utility. Specify the --schema option to specify the schema(s) to be backed up. For example, to backup the "sales" and "production" schemas in the AdventureWorks database:

```
pg_dump -U postgres -h localhost -F c -b -v -f
/path/to/schema/backup/adventureworks_sales_production.backup -n sales -n
production adventureworks
```

This will create a compressed backup file in the specified directory that contains the specified schemas.

Verify the Backup

Verify the integrity of the backup file by restoring it to a test database and running some test queries to ensure that the schema(s) are present and functional.

By using a schema-level backup, you can selectively backup parts of your PostgreSQL database and save time and storage space. Note that it's important to test the backup and restore process thoroughly to ensure that it's working correctly. Also, it's recommended to perform regular full backups in addition to schema-level backups to ensure that you have a complete backup of your database.

Recipe#7: Perform Backup Monitoring using pg_stat_activity

You can monitor the backup of the AdventureWorks database in PostgreSQL 15 using the pg_stat_activity view. This view displays information about all active connections and transactions in the PostgreSQL server, including backup processes.

Below is how to use pg_stat_activity to monitor the backup of the AdventureWorks database:

Connect to Database

Connect to the AdventureWorks database using a database client or the psql utility.

Query pg_stat_activity

Execute the following query to view all active connections and transactions in the PostgreSQL server:

```
SELECT * FROM pg_stat_activity;
```

This will display information about all active connections and transactions in the server, including backup processes.

Filter by Backup Process

To filter the output by backup process, you can search for queries that contain the pg_dump or pg_dumpall command in the query column of the pg_stat_activity view. For example:

```
SELECT * FROM pg_stat_activity WHERE query LIKE 'pg_dump%' OR
query LIKE 'pg_dumpall%';
```

This will display information about all backup processes that are currently running in the server.

Monitor Backup Progress

To monitor the progress of a specific backup process, you can look at the query column to identify the backup command and the state column to identify the current state of the backup process. For example, a state of "active" indicates that the backup process is still running, while a state of "idle" indicates that the backup process has completed.

By using pg_stat_activity to monitor the backup of the AdventureWorks database, you can ensure that the backup process is running correctly and track the progress of the backup. Note that it's important to monitor the backup process regularly and verify that the backup files are being created correctly.

CHAPTER 11: EXPLORING DATABASE RECOVERY & RESTORATION METHODS

Recipe#1: Perform Full and PITR Recovery

Full Recovery

Full recovery involves restoring the database from a complete backup. To perform a full recovery of a PostgreSQL database, follow these steps:

Ensure you have a complete backup of the database. PostgreSQL has a built-in tool called pg_dump that you can use to create a backup. If you already have a backup, skip this step. If not, run the following command:

```
pg_dump -U your_user -W -F t your_database > backup.tar
```

Replace your_user and your_database with the appropriate values for your setup.

Drop the existing database to prepare for the recovery:

```
dropdb -U your_user your_database
```

Create a new, empty database with the same name as the original:

```
createdb -U your_user your_database
```

Restore the backup to the newly created database:

```
pg_restore -U your_user -d your_database -F t backup.tar
```

After the command completes, your database should be fully recovered.

Point-in-Time Recovery (PITR)

PITR allows you to restore your database to a specific point in time. To perform PITR for a PostgreSQL database, follow these steps:

Configure your PostgreSQL instance for continuous archiving by setting the following parameters in the postgresql.conf file:

```
wal_level = replica
```

```
archive_mode = on
archive_command = 'cp %p /path/to/archive/%f'
```

The wal_level setting must be set to replica to enable archiving. The archive_mode setting must be set to on to turn on archiving. The archive_command setting specifies the command to use for archiving. This command should copy the WAL file %p to the archive directory /path/to/archive/%f, where %f is the filename of the WAL file. You should replace /path/to/archive/ with the path to the directory where you want to store the archive files.

Restart the PostgreSQL server to apply the new configuration.

Create a base backup of the database using pg_basebackup. This creates a snapshot of the database at a specific point in time. Run the following command:

```
pg_basebackup -U your_user -D /path/to/backup -Ft -Xs -P
```

Replace your_user with the appropriate value for your setup, and /path/to/backup with the path to the directory where you want to store the backup.

After the base backup is created, start the PostgreSQL server in recovery mode by creating a recovery.conf file in the data directory with the following contents:

```
standby_mode = on
primary_conninfo = 'host=localhost port=5432 user=your_user'
restore_command = 'cp /path/to/archive/%f "%p"'
recovery_target_time = 'YYYY-MM-DD HH:MI:SS'
```

Replace your_user with the appropriate value for your setup. The primary_conninfo setting specifies the connection information for the primary server, which is used to fetch WAL files.

The restore_command setting specifies how to restore archived WAL files. The recovery_target_time setting specifies the time to recover to.

Start the PostgreSQL server in recovery mode:

```
pg_ctl start -D /path/to/data -w -t 600
```

Replace /path/to/data with the path to the data directory for the PostgreSQL instance.

After the server starts, it will apply WAL files to bring the database to the specified point in time. Once it reaches the target time, it will stop applying WAL files and the database will be in a consistent state at that time. You can then use the database normally.

Note: When performing PITR, it's important to keep the WAL archive files in a safe place, as they are required for the recovery process.

Recipe#2: Restore Database using Barman

Barman is an open-source backup and recovery tool for PostgreSQL. It provides a simple and reliable solution for backing up and restoring PostgreSQL databases, including support for Point-in-Time Recovery (PITR). In this recipe, I will describe how to restore the given database using Barman.

Before proceeding with the restore process, you need to confirm that you have:

Installed Barman and configured it to manage the backups of your PostgreSQL database.

Taken a backup of your PostgreSQL database using Barman.

Assuming that you have met the above requirements, follow the steps below to restore the database using Barman:

Check the status of the backups in Barman by running the following command:

```
barman list-backup your_database
```

This will show you a list of backups that have been taken for your database, along with their status.

Select the backup that you want to restore and mark it as "restored" by running the following command:

```
barman mark-restore your_database backup_id
```

Replace backup_id with the ID of the backup that you want to restore. This command tells Barman to mark the backup as "restored" so that it will not be used for future PITR operations.

Create a temporary directory for the restore process:

mkdir /path/to/restore

Replace /path/to/restore with the path to the directory where you want to store the restored database.

Restore the base backup by running the following command:

barman recover --remote-ssh-command "ssh user@your_server" --target-directory /path/to/restore your_database backup_id

Replace user@your_server with the SSH connection information for your PostgreSQL server, /path/to/restore with the path to the directory where you want to restore the database, your_database with the name of your PostgreSQL database, and backup_id with the ID of the backup that you want to restore. This command tells Barman to restore the base backup for your database to the specified directory.

After the base backup is restored, start the PostgreSQL server in recovery mode:

pg_ctl -D /path/to/restore start

Replace /path/to/restore with the path to the directory where you restored the database.

Wait for the PostgreSQL server to apply the archived WAL files to the restored database. You can monitor the progress of the recovery process by running the following command:

tail -f /path/to/restore/pg_log/postgresql-<date>.log

Replace <date> with the date on which you restored the database. This command will show you the latest entries in the PostgreSQL log file, which will include information about the recovery process.

Once the recovery process is complete, stop the PostgreSQL server:

pg_ctl -D /path/to/restore stop

Copy the restored database to the original PostgreSQL data directory:

rsync -av /path/to/restore/ /var/lib/postgresql/data/

Replace /path/to/restore with the path to the directory where you restored the database, and /var/lib/postgresql/data/ with the path to the PostgreSQL data directory on your server.

Change the ownership of the data directory to the PostgreSQL user:

chown -R postgres:postgres /var/lib/postgresql/data/

This command ensures that the PostgreSQL user has the necessary permissions to access the restored database.

Start the PostgreSQL server:

systemctl start postgresql

Verify that the database is accessible and working properly by connecting to it with a PostgreSQL client:

psql -U postgres your_database

This command will connect you to the restored database using the PostgreSQL client. You can then execute SQL commands to verify that the data is intact.

Recipe#3: Perform Incremental/Differential Restore

Barman provides support for incremental and differential backups, which can be used to reduce the amount of data that needs to be restored during a recovery operation. In this recipe, I will describe how to perform an incremental or differential restore of the adventureworks database using Barman.

Assuming that you have already taken a full backup of the adventureworks database and at least one incremental or differential backup, follow the steps below to perform an incremental or differential restore:

Check the status of the backups in Barman by running the following command:

barman list-backup adventureworks

This will show you a list of backups that have been taken for the adventureworks database, along with their status.

Select the full backup that you want to restore and mark it as "restored" by running the following command:

barman mark-restore adventureworks full_backup_id

Replace full_backup_id with the ID of the full backup that you want to restore. This command tells Barman to mark the full backup as "restored" so that it will not be used for future PITR operations.

Create a temporary directory for the restore process:

mkdir /path/to/restore

Replace /path/to/restore with the path to the directory where you want to store the restored database.

Restore the full backup by running the following command:

barman recover --remote-ssh-command "ssh user@your_server" --target-directory /path/to/restore adventureworks full_backup_id

Replace user@your_server with the SSH connection information for your PostgreSQL server, /path/to/restore with the path to the directory where you want to restore the database, adventureworks with the name of your PostgreSQL database, and full_backup_id with the ID of the full backup that you want to restore. This command tells Barman to restore the full backup for your database to the specified directory.

After the full backup is restored, start the PostgreSQL server in recovery mode:

```
pg_ctl -D /path/to/restore start
```

Replace /path/to/restore with the path to the directory where you restored the database.

Wait for the PostgreSQL server to apply the archived WAL files to the restored database. You can monitor the progress of the recovery process by running the following command:

```
tail -f /path/to/restore/pg_log/postgresql-<date>.log
```

Replace <date> with the date on which you restored the database. This command will show you the latest entries in the PostgreSQL log file, which will include information about the recovery process.

Once the recovery process is complete, stop the PostgreSQL server:

```
pg_ctl -D /path/to/restore stop
```

Copy the restored database to the original PostgreSQL data directory:

```
rsync -av /path/to/restore/ /var/lib/postgresql/data/
```

Replace /path/to/restore with the path to the directory where you restored the database, and /var/lib/postgresql/data/ with the path to the PostgreSQL data directory on your server.

Change the ownership of the data directory to the PostgreSQL user:

```
chown -R postgres:postgres /var/lib/postgresql/data/
```

This command ensures that the PostgreSQL user has the necessary permissions to access the restored database.

Start the PostgreSQL server:

```
systemctl start postgresql
```

If you have taken an incremental or differential backup after the full backup, mark it as "restored" by running the following command:

barman mark-restore adventureworks incremental_backup_id

Replace incremental_backup_id with the ID of the incremental or differential backup that you want to restore. This command tells Barman to mark the backup as "restored" so that it will not be used for future PITR operations.

Restore the incremental or differential backup by running the following command:

barman recover --remote-ssh-command "ssh user@your_server" --target-directory /path/to/restore --delta /path/to/full/backup/incremental_backup_id.tar.gz adventureworks incremental_backup_id

Replace user@your_server with the SSH connection information for your PostgreSQL server, /path/to/restore with the path to the directory where you want to restore the database, adventureworks with the name of your PostgreSQL database, incremental_backup_id with the ID of the incremental or differential backup that you want to restore, and /path/to/full/backup/incremental_backup_id.tar.gz with the path to the full backup that the incremental or differential backup is based on. This command tells Barman to restore the incremental or differential backup for your database to the specified directory, using the full backup as the base.

After the incremental or differential backup is restored, start the PostgreSQL server in recovery mode:

pg_ctl -D /path/to/restore start

Wait for the PostgreSQL server to apply the archived WAL files to the restored database. You can monitor the progress of the recovery process by running the following command:

tail -f /path/to/restore/pg_log/postgresql-<date>.log

Once the recovery process is complete, stop the PostgreSQL server:

pg_ctl -D /path/to/restore stop

Copy the restored database to the original PostgreSQL data directory:

rsync -av /path/to/restore/ /var/lib/postgresql/data/

Replace /path/to/restore with the path to the directory where you restored the database, and /var/lib/postgresql/data/ with the path to the PostgreSQL data directory on your server.

Change the ownership of the data directory to the PostgreSQL user:

chown -R postgres:postgres /var/lib/postgresql/data/

Start the PostgreSQL server:

systemctl start postgresql

Verify that the database is accessible and working properly by connecting to it with a PostgreSQL client:

psql -U postgres adventureworks

This command will connect you to the restored database using the PostgreSQL client. You can then execute SQL commands to verify that the data is intact.

By following all the above lengthy steps, You have successfully performed an incremental or differential restore of the adventureworks database using Barman.

Recipe#4: Working with Tablespace Recovery

Tablespaces in PostgreSQL are a way of organizing database objects into separate directories on disk. They provide a mechanism for controlling the physical layout of database files and can be used to improve performance and manageability. Barman supports tablespace recovery, which allows you to restore individual tablespaces in case of a disaster. In this recipe, I will describe how to work with tablespace recovery for the adventureworks database using Barman.

Assuming that you have already taken a backup of the adventureworks database that includes tablespaces, follow the steps below to perform tablespace recovery:

Check the status of the backups in Barman by running the following command:

barman list-backup adventureworks

This will show you a list of backups that have been taken for the adventureworks database, along with their status.

Select the backup that you want to restore and mark it as "restored" by running the following command:

barman mark-restore adventureworks backup_id

Replace backup_id with the ID of the backup that you want to restore. This command tells Barman to mark the backup as "restored" so that it will not be used for future PITR operations.

Create a temporary directory for the restore process:

mkdir /path/to/restore

Replace /path/to/restore with the path to the directory where you want to store the restored tablespaces.

Restore the tablespaces by running the following command:

barman recover-tablespace --remote-ssh-command "ssh user@your_server" --target-directory /path/to/restore --tablespace-name your_tablespace_name adventureworks backup_id

Replace user@your_server with the SSH connection information for your PostgreSQL server, /path/to/restore with the path to the directory where you want to restore the tablespaces, your_tablespace_name with the name of the tablespace that you want to restore, adventureworks with the name of your PostgreSQL database, and backup_id with the ID of the backup that you want to restore. This command tells Barman to restore the specified tablespace for your database to the specified directory.

After the tablespaces are restored, copy them to the original directory on disk:

```
rsync -av /path/to/restore/ /var/lib/postgresql/data/pg_tblspc/
```

Replace /path/to/restore with the path to the directory where you restored the tablespaces, and /var/lib/postgresql/data/pg_tblspc/ with the path to the PostgreSQL tablespace directory on your server.

Change the ownership of the tablespace directory to the PostgreSQL user:

```
chown -R postgres:postgres /var/lib/postgresql/data/pg_tblspc/
```

Restart the PostgreSQL server to apply the changes:

```
systemctl restart postgresql
```

By now, You have successfully performed tablespace recovery for the adventureworks database using Barman.

Recipe#5: Working with Tables Recovery

In PostgreSQL, tables are the fundamental objects that store data in a database. In case of a disaster, it may be necessary to restore individual tables from a backup. Barman supports table-level recovery, which allows you to restore individual tables from a backup without affecting the rest of the database. In this recipe, I will describe how to work with table recovery for the adventureworks database using Barman.

Assuming that you have already taken a backup of the adventureworks database that includes the tables that you want to restore, follow the steps below to perform table recovery:

Check the status of the backups in Barman by running the following command:

barman list-backup adventureworks

This will show you a list of backups that have been taken for the adventureworks database, along with their status.

Select the backup that you want to restore and mark it as "restored" by running the following command:

barman mark-restore adventureworks backup_id

Replace backup_id with the ID of the backup that you want to restore. This command tells Barman to mark the backup as "restored" so that it will not be used for future PITR operations.

Create a temporary directory for the restore process:

mkdir /path/to/restore

Replace /path/to/restore with the path to the directory where you want to store the restored table.

Restore the table by running the following command:

barman recover-table --remote-ssh-command "ssh user@your_server" --target-directory /path/to/restore --tablespace-name your_tablespace_name adventureworks backup_id your_table_name

Replace user@your_server with the SSH connection information for your PostgreSQL server, /path/to/restore with the path to the directory where you want to restore the table, your_tablespace_name with the name of the tablespace that contains the table you want to restore, adventureworks with the name of your PostgreSQL database, backup_id with the ID of the backup that you want to restore, and your_table_name with the name of the table that you want to restore. This command tells Barman to restore the specified table for your database to the specified directory.

After the table is restored, create a new table with the same schema in the database:

```
psql -U postgres -d adventureworks -c "CREATE TABLE your_table_name
(LIKE your_table_name INCLUDING ALL);"
```

Replace your_table_name with the name of the table that you want to restore.

Use the pg_restore utility to load the data from the restored table into the new table:

```
pg_restore --data-only --table=your_table_name --dbname=adventureworks
/path/to/restore/your_table_name.sql
```

Replace your_table_name with the name of the table that you want to restore, /path/to/restore with the path to the directory where you restored the table, and adventureworks with the name of your PostgreSQL database.

Verify that the data is restored correctly by querying the new table:

```
psql -U postgres -d adventureworks -c "SELECT COUNT(*) FROM
your_table_name;"
```

Replace your_table_name with the name of the table that you restored and the table recovery for the adventureworks database using Barman is successful.

Recipe#6: Working with Schema Level Restore

In PostgreSQL, a schema is a logical container for database objects such as tables, views, and functions. In case of a disaster, it may be necessary to restore individual schemas from a backup. Barman supports schema-level recovery, which allows you to restore individual schemas from a backup without affecting the rest of the database. In this recipe, I will describe how to work with schema-level restore for the adventureworks database using Barman.

Assuming that you have already taken a backup of the adventureworks database that includes the schema that you want to restore, follow the steps below to perform schema-level restore:

Check the status of the backups in Barman by running the following command:

barman list-backup adventureworks

This will show you a list of backups that have been taken for the adventureworks database, along with their status.

Select the backup that you want to restore and mark it as "restored" by running the following command:

barman mark-restore adventureworks backup_id

Replace backup_id with the ID of the backup that you want to restore. This command tells Barman to mark the backup as "restored" so that it will not be used for future PITR operations.

Create a temporary directory for the restore process:

mkdir /path/to/restore

Replace /path/to/restore with the path to the directory where you want to store the restored schema.

Restore the schema by running the following command:

barman recover-schema --remote-ssh-command "ssh user@your_server" --target-directory /path/to/restore --tablespace-name your_tablespace_name adventureworks backup_id your_schema_name

Replace user@your_server with the SSH connection information for your PostgreSQL server, /path/to/restore with the path to the directory where you want to restore the schema, your_tablespace_name with the name of the tablespace that contains the schema you want to restore, adventureworks with the name of your PostgreSQL database, backup_id with the ID of the backup that you want to restore, and your_schema_name with the name of the schema that you want to restore. This command tells Barman to restore the specified schema for your database to the specified directory.

After the schema is restored, use the pg_restore utility to create a new schema in the database with the same name:

```
pg_restore --schema-only --dbname=adventureworks
/path/to/restore/your_schema_name.sql
```

Replace /path/to/restore with the path to the directory where you restored the schema, and adventureworks with the name of your PostgreSQL database.

Verify that the schema is restored correctly by querying the new schema:

```
psql -U postgres -d adventureworks -c "\d your_schema_name.*;"
```

Replace your_schema_name with the name of the schema that you restored and the schema-level restore is complete.

Recipe#7: Monitor Restore Operations

Barman provides several options for monitoring restore operations in progress. In this recipe, I will describe how to monitor restore operations for the adventureworks database using Barman.

Check the status of the restore operation by running the following command:

```
barman list-restore adventureworks
```

This will show you a list of all restores that are in progress or have been completed for the adventureworks database. The output will include the status of each restore, the name of the backup being restored, and the target directory for the restore.

To monitor the progress of a restore operation, run the following command:

```
barman show-restore adventureworks restore_id
```

Replace restore_id with the ID of the restore operation that you want to monitor. This command will show you the status of the restore operation, the name of the backup being restored, and the target directory for the restore. It will also show you the progress of the restore operation, including the number of files that have been restored and the estimated time remaining.

To view the log messages for a restore operation, run the following command:

barman show-restore-logs adventureworks restore_id

Replace restore_id with the ID of the restore operation that you want to monitor. This command will show you the log messages for the restore operation, including any errors or warnings that were encountered during the restore process.

If you want to stop a restore operation that is in progress, run the following command:

barman stop-restore adventureworks restore_id

Replace restore_id with the ID of the restore operation that you want to stop. This command will stop the restore operation and remove the restore lock on the backup that was being restored. By this, you have learned how to monitor restore operations using Barman.

Recipe#8: Working with Recovery Mode

In Barman, recovery mode is a state in which the PostgreSQL server is running using data that has been recovered from a backup. In this mode, you can perform several tasks, including testing the restored data and performing point-in-time recovery operations. In this recipe, I will describe how to work with recovery mode for the adventureworks database using Barman.

Assuming that you have already restored the adventureworks database using Barman, follow the steps below to start the PostgreSQL server in recovery mode:

Open the postgresql.conf file located in the data directory of your PostgreSQL installation:

nano /var/lib/postgresql/data/postgresql.conf

Uncomment the following lines in the file:

# recovery.conf
include_dir = 'conf.d'

Save and close the file.

Create a recovery.conf file in the conf.d directory:

nano /var/lib/postgresql/data/conf.d/recovery.conf

Add the following lines to the file:

standby_mode = 'on'
primary_conninfo = 'host=your_server port=5432 user=your_user
password=your_password'
restore_command = 'barman-wal-restore your_barman_server adventureworks
%f %p'
trigger_file = '/var/lib/postgresql/data/failover.trigger'

Replace your_server with the IP address or hostname of your PostgreSQL server, your_user and your_password with the PostgreSQL user credentials that you want to use for the recovery process, your_barman_server with the hostname or IP address of your Barman server, and /var/lib/postgresql/data/failover.trigger with the path to the failover trigger file.

The restore_command parameter specifies the command that will be used to retrieve WAL files from Barman during the recovery process. %f and %p are placeholders for the WAL file name and path, respectively.

Save and close the recovery.conf file.

Create the failover trigger file:

touch /var/lib/postgresql/data/failover.trigger

Start the PostgreSQL server in recovery mode:

pg_ctl -D /var/lib/postgresql/data/ -l /var/lib/postgresql/data/logfile start

Verify that the PostgreSQL server is running in recovery mode:

```
psql -U postgres -c "SELECT pg_is_in_recovery();"
```

The output should be t, indicating that the PostgreSQL server is running in recovery mode.

Recipe#9: Working with Recovery Target Options

In PostgreSQL, recovery target options are parameters that can be used to specify the recovery target for a point-in-time recovery operation. These options allow you to recover the database to a specific point in time or up to a certain transaction ID. In this recipe, I will describe how to work with recovery target options for the adventureworks database using Barman.

Assuming that you have already restored the adventureworks database using Barman and started the PostgreSQL server in recovery mode, follow the steps below to work with recovery target options:

To recover the database up to a specific point in time, add the following line to the recovery.conf file:

```
recovery_target_time = 'YYYY-MM-DD HH:MI:SS'
```

Replace YYYY-MM-DD HH:MI:SS with the date and time up to which you want to recover the database.

To recover the database up to a specific transaction ID, add the following line to the recovery.conf file:

```
recovery_target_xid = 'transaction_ID'
```

Replace transaction_ID with the transaction ID up to which you want to recover the database.

To recover the database up to the last transaction that was committed before a specific point in time, add the following line to the recovery.conf file:

```
recovery_target_time = 'YYYY-MM-DD HH:MI:SS'
```

recovery_target_inclusive = 'false'

Replace YYYY-MM-DD HH:MI:SS with the date and time before which you want to recover the database.

To recover the database to the end of the WAL logs, add the following line to the recovery.conf file:

recovery_target = 'immediate'

This will recover the database up to the end of the WAL logs, which is the point at which the last backup was taken.

Save and close the recovery.conf file.

Restart the PostgreSQL server in recovery mode:

pg_ctl -D /var/lib/postgresql/data/ -l /var/lib/postgresql/data/logfile restart

Verify that the PostgreSQL server is running in recovery mode:

psql -U postgres -c "SELECT pg_is_in_recovery();"

The output should be t, indicating that the PostgreSQL server is running in recovery mode.

CHAPTER 12: PROMETHEUS & CONTINUOUS MONITORING

Recipe#1: Installing and Configuring Prometheus

Prometheus is a powerful monitoring system that collects and stores metrics from various sources and allows you to query and visualize the data. In this recipe, I will describe how to install and configure Prometheus for the adventureworks database.

Install Prometheus by downloading the latest release from the official website:

```
wget
https://github.com/prometheus/prometheus/releases/download/v2.30.3/prometh
eus-2.30.3.linux-amd64.tar.gz
tar xvfz prometheus-2.30.3.linux-amd64.tar.gz
```

This will download and extract the Prometheus binary to the current directory.

Configure Prometheus by editing the prometheus.yml file:

```
nano prometheus-2.30.3.linux-amd64/prometheus.yml
```

Add the following lines to the file:

```
global:
  scrape_interval: 15s
scrape_configs:
  - job_name: 'postgres'
    static_configs:
      - targets: ['localhost:9090']
    metrics_path: '/metrics'
    params:
      query: |
        postgres_exporter_database_size_bytes{database="adventureworks"}
        postgres_exporter_table_size_bytes{database="adventureworks"}
```

This configuration file tells Prometheus to scrape metrics from the PostgreSQL server running on the local machine on port 9090. It also specifies the metrics to collect, which include the size of the adventureworks database and tables.

Save and close the prometheus.yml file.

Start the Prometheus server:

```
prometheus-2.30.3.linux-amd64/prometheus --config.file=prometheus-2.30.3.linux-amd64/prometheus.yml
```

Verify that the Prometheus server is running by accessing the web interface:

```
http://localhost:9090
```

This will open the Prometheus web interface, where you can view and query the collected metrics.

Recipe#2: Real-time Monitoring using Prometheus

Once you have installed and configured Prometheus for the adventureworks database, you can use it to do real-time monitoring of the database by querying the collected metrics. In this recipe, I will describe how to use Prometheus to perform real-time monitoring of the adventureworks database.

Access the Prometheus web interface:

```
http://localhost:9090
```

Navigate to the "Graph" section of the web interface.

In the "Expression" input box, enter the following query to display the size of the adventureworks database:

```
postgres_exporter_database_size_bytes{database="adventureworks"}
```

This query will display the size of the adventureworks database in bytes.

In the "Expression" input box, enter the following query to display the size of the salesorderdetail table in the adventureworks database:

```
postgres_exporter_table_size_bytes{database="adventureworks",
table="salesorderdetail"}
```

This query will display the size of the salesorderdetail table in bytes.

To monitor the rate of queries being executed on the adventureworks database, enter the following query in the "Expression" input box:

```
rate(pg_stat_database_xact_commit{datname='adventureworks'}[5m])
```

This query will display the rate of transactions being committed to the adventureworks database over the last 5 minutes.

To monitor the memory usage of the PostgreSQL server, enter the following query in the "Expression" input box:

```
node_memory_MemTotal - node_memory_MemFree - node_memory_Buffers
- node_memory_Cached
```

This query will display the amount of memory being used by the PostgreSQL server.

You can also create custom queries to monitor specific aspects of the adventureworks database, such as the number of orders placed or the average order amount.

By now, you have successfully used Prometheus to perform real-time monitoring of the adventureworks database. By querying the collected metrics, you can gain insights into the performance and usage of the database, and take proactive measures to optimize its performance.

Recipe#3: Using Statistic Collector and Analyzer

PostgreSQL's statistics collector and analyzer are powerful tools that allow you to collect and analyze performance metrics and usage statistics for your database. In this recipe, I will describe how to use the statistics collector and analyzer for the adventureworks database.

Enable the statistics collector by adding the following line to the postgresql.conf file:

```
#stats_collector = off
stats_collector = on
```

This will enable the statistics collector, which will start collecting metrics about the database's performance and usage.

Restart the PostgreSQL server for the changes to take effect:

```
systemctl restart postgresql.service
```

Verify that the statistics collector is running by checking the contents of the pg_stat directory:

```
ls /var/lib/postgresql/data/pg_stat/
```

This directory should contain several files that correspond to different aspects of the database's performance, such as pg_stat_database, pg_stat_activity, and pg_stat_user_tables.

Use the pg_stat_database view to monitor database-level statistics, such as the number of queries being executed and the amount of data being read and written:

```
SELECT datname, numbackends, xact_commit, xact_rollback, blks_read,
blks_hit FROM pg_stat_database WHERE datname='adventureworks';
```

This query will display the number of active connections, transactions committed and rolled back, and the number of blocks read and hit for the adventureworks database.

Use the pg_stat_user_tables view to monitor table-level statistics, such as the number of queries being executed on a specific table and the amount of data being read and written:

```
SELECT relname, seq_scan, seq_tup_read, idx_scan, idx_tup_fetch, n_tup_ins,
n_tup_upd, n_tup_del FROM pg_stat_user_tables WHERE
schemaname='public' AND relname='salesorderdetail';
```

This query will display the number of sequential and index scans and tuples read for the salesorderdetail table in the public schema.

Use the pg_stat_activity view to monitor the current activity on the PostgreSQL server, including the queries being executed and the users connected to the server:

```
SELECT datname, usename, query FROM pg_stat_activity WHERE
datname='adventureworks';
```

This query will display the active queries being executed on the adventureworks database and the users connected to the server. By analyzing these metrics, you can identify performance bottlenecks and optimize the database's configuration and queries for better performance.

Recipe#4: Using Prometheus to Monitor Active Session

You can use Prometheus to monitor the number of active sessions on the PostgreSQL server running the adventureworks database. To do this, you can use the pg_stat_activity view in conjunction with Prometheus's postgres_exporter module, which exposes PostgreSQL metrics in a format that can be consumed by Prometheus. In this recipe, I will describe how to use Prometheus to monitor active sessions for the adventureworks database.

Install the postgres_exporter module by following the installation instructions provided in the official documentation:

```
git clone https://github.com/wrouesnel/postgres_exporter.git
cd postgres_exporter
```

This will download and compile the postgres_exporter module.

Start the postgres_exporter module:

```
./postgres_exporter --extend.query-path=/path/to/custom/queries --web.listen-address=":9187" --disable-default-metrics
```

This will start the postgres_exporter module on port 9187 and enable it to run custom queries located in the specified directory.

Configure Prometheus to scrape metrics from the postgres_exporter module:

```
global:
  scrape_interval: 15s
scrape_configs:
  - job_name: 'postgres_exporter'
    static_configs:
      - targets: ['localhost:9187']
```

Save and close the prometheus.yml file.

Restart the Prometheus server:

```
prometheus --config.file=prometheus.yml
```

Verify that Prometheus is scraping metrics from the postgres_exporter module by accessing the Prometheus web interface:

```
http://localhost:9090
```

Navigate to the "Graph" section of the web interface.

In the "Expression" input box, enter the following query to display the number of active sessions on the PostgreSQL server:

```
postgresql_activity_count
```

This query will display the number of active sessions on the PostgreSQL server, including the adventureworks database.

Recipe#5: Parse Query String

In PostgreSQL, you can parse a query string using the pg_query_parse() function, which returns a parse tree for the specified query. The parse tree contains information about the syntax and structure of the query, including the tables, columns, and conditions used in the query. In this recipe, I will describe how to parse a query string for the adventureworks database.

Connect to the adventureworks database using psql:

psql -U postgres -d adventureworks

Enter the following command to enable the pg_stat_statements extension, which provides statistics about the execution of SQL statements on the server:

CREATE EXTENSION IF NOT EXISTS pg_stat_statements;

Execute some SQL statements on the adventureworks database to populate the pg_stat_statements view:

SELECT * FROM salesorderdetail;
SELECT * FROM salesorderheader WHERE orderdate >= '2007-01-01';

Enter the following command to parse a query string:

SELECT * FROM pg_query_parse('SELECT * FROM salesorderdetail;');

This command will return a parse tree for the specified query, which contains information about the tables and columns used in the query.

To parse a more complex query, enter the following command:

SELECT * FROM pg_query_parse('SELECT * FROM salesorderheader
WHERE orderdate >= "2007-01-01" ORDER BY orderdate DESC LIMIT 10;');

This command will return a parse tree for the specified query, which includes information about the conditions, sorting, and limiting used in the query. You have successfully parsed a query string for the adventureworks database using the pg_query_parse() function. By analyzing the parse tree, you can gain insights into the syntax and structure of the query, which can help you optimize the database's configuration and queries for better performance.

Recipe#6: Use Database Connection Pooling

Database connection pooling is a technique that allows multiple client applications to share a pool of database connections, which can improve the performance and scalability of the database. In PostgreSQL, you can use various connection pooling solutions to implement connection pooling for the adventureworks database, such as PgBouncer and pgpool-II. In this recipe, I will describe how to use PgBouncer to implement database connection pooling for the adventureworks database.

Install PgBouncer by following the installation instructions provided in the official documentation:

sudo apt-get install pgbouncer

Configure PgBouncer by editing the pgbouncer.ini file:

nano /etc/pgbouncer/pgbouncer.ini

Set the following parameters in the [databases] section of the pgbouncer.ini file:

[databases]
adventureworks = host=localhost port=5432 dbname=adventureworks
user=postgres password=postgres

This specifies the connection details for the adventureworks database.

Set the following parameters in the [pgbouncer] section of the pgbouncer.ini file:

[pgbouncer]
listen_addr = *

```
listen_port = 6432
auth_type = md5
auth_file = /etc/pgbouncer/userlist.txt
server_reset_query = DISCARD ALL
max_client_conn = 100
default_pool_size = 20
```

This specifies the settings for the PgBouncer instance, such as the listening address and port, authentication type and file, maximum number of client connections, and default pool size.

Create the userlist.txt file and add the following line to it:

```
"postgres" "postgres"
```

This specifies the authentication credentials for the PostgreSQL user.

Start the PgBouncer server:

```
pgbouncer -d /etc/pgbouncer/pgbouncer.ini
```

Connect to the adventureworks database using PgBouncer by specifying the PgBouncer server address and port in the connection string:

```
psql -U postgres -h localhost -p 6432 -d adventureworks
```

This will connect to the adventureworks database through the PgBouncer connection pool. You have successfully implemented database connection pooling for the adventureworks database using PgBouncer. By sharing a pool of database connections, you can reduce the overhead of establishing new connections and improve the performance and scalability of the database.

Recipe#7: Vacuum amd Bloat

In PostgreSQL, the VACUUM command is used to reclaim disk space and optimize the performance of the database by removing dead rows and updating the table statistics. Bloat refs to the excessive usage of disk space by the database, which can occur due to various reasons such as unoptimized queries, long-running transactions, and inefficient maintenance operations. In this recipe, I will describe in detail about vacuum and bloat for the adventureworks database.

Understanding Vacuum

The VACUUM command is used to reclaim disk space and optimize the performance of the database by removing dead rows and updating the table statistics. Dead rows are rows that are no longer needed and can be safely removed from the table.

The VACUUM command performs the following operations:
- Removes dead rows from the table.
- Updates the table statistics, which are used by the PostgreSQL query planner to optimize queries.
- Reclaims disk space by compacting the table.

The VACUUM command can be run on a specific table, a specific schema, or the entire database.

Understanding Bloat

Bloat refers to the excessive usage of disk space by the database, which can occur due to various reasons such as unoptimized queries, long-running transactions, and inefficient maintenance operations. Bloat can cause performance degradation and disk space exhaustion, and should be addressed through regular maintenance operations such as VACUUM and REINDEX.

Bloat can occur in the following forms:
- Table bloat: Occurs when a table has more dead rows than live rows, resulting in inefficient disk usage and slow queries.
- Index bloat: Occurs when an index has become too large due to excessive fragmentation or redundant data, resulting in slow queries and excessive disk usage.
- Database bloat: Occurs when the database has become too large due to excessive table and index bloat, resulting in slow queries, long backup times, and excessive disk usage.

Addressing Bloat

Bloat can be addressed through regular maintenance operations such as VACUUM and REINDEX, which reclaim disk space and optimize the performance of the database.

The following steps can be taken to address bloat in the adventureworks database:

- Use the VACUUM command to reclaim disk space and optimize the performance of the database by removing dead rows and updating the table statistics.
- Use the ANALYZE command to update the table statistics and optimize the query planner.
- Use the REINDEX command to rebuild indexes that have become bloated due to excessive fragmentation or redundant data.
- Monitor the disk usage of the database and ensure that it does not exceed the available disk space.
- Tune the queries and transactions to reduce the usage of disk space and optimize the performance of the database.

To summarize, vacuum and bloat are critical concepts in PostgreSQL that should be understood and addressed through regular maintenance operations to ensure optimal performance and disk space usage of the adventureworks database.

Recipe#8: Using 'fsync'

In PostgreSQL, fsync is a configuration parameter that determines whether or not the database writes data to disk immediately after each transaction commit. fsync is an important parameter because it affects the durability and reliability of the database, as well as its performance.

When fsync is enabled, the database writes data to disk immediately after each transaction commit, ensuring that the data is safely stored on disk and is recoverable in the event of a system crash or power failure. However, this can impact performance, as the write operations can be slow and cause delays in the transaction processing.

When fsync is disabled, the database does not write data to disk immediately after each transaction commit, which can improve performance but can also increase the risk of data loss or corruption in the event of a system crash or power failure. Therefore, it is important to carefully consider the implications of enabling or disabling fsync based on the specific requirements and constraints of your application.

To use fsync for the adventureworks database, you can follow these steps:

Connect to the adventureworks database using psql:

```
psql -U postgres -d adventureworks
```

Enter the following command to view the current value of the fsync parameter:

SHOW fsync;

This command will display the current value of the fsync parameter, which is either on or off.

Enter the following command to change the value of the fsync parameter:

SET fsync TO off;

This command will disable the fsync parameter, which can improve performance but can also increase the risk of data loss or corruption in the event of a system crash or power failure.

Enter the following command to verify that the fsync parameter has been disabled:

SHOW fsync;

This command will display the current value of the fsync parameter, which should be off.

To enable fsync again, enter the following command:

SET fsync TO on;

This command will enable the fsync parameter, which ensures that the data is safely stored on disk and is recoverable in the event of a system crash or power failure.

Enter the following command to verify that the fsync parameter has been enabled:

SHOW fsync;

This command will display the current value of the fsync parameter, which should be on. By carefully considering the implications of enabling or disabling fsync, you can ensure optimal performance and data safety for your application.

CHAPTER 13: DEBUGGING POSTGRESQL

Recipe#1: Benchmarking and its Importance

Benchmarking is the process of measuring and evaluating the performance of a system under controlled conditions. In the context of PostgreSQL, benchmarking is an important tool for measuring the performance and scalability of the database, as well as identifying and resolving performance bottlenecks and other issues. In this recipe, I will describe in detail about benchmarking and its importance for PostgreSQL performance.

Understanding Benchmarking

Benchmarking involves measuring and evaluating the performance of a system under controlled conditions, such as by running a set of predefined workloads and measuring the response times and throughput of the system. Benchmarking can be used to identify performance bottlenecks, evaluate the scalability of the system, and compare the performance of different configurations or systems.

In the context of PostgreSQL, benchmarking involves running a set of predefined queries or transactions on the database and measuring the response times, throughput, and other performance metrics. Benchmarking can be performed using various tools and frameworks, such as pgbench, HammerDB, and Apache JMeter.

Importance of Benchmarking for PostgreSQL Performance

Benchmarking is an important tool for measuring and evaluating the performance of the PostgreSQL database, as well as identifying and resolving performance bottlenecks and other issues.

The following are some of the key benefits of benchmarking for PostgreSQL performance:
- Identifying performance bottlenecks: By running a set of predefined workloads on the database and measuring the response times and throughput, benchmarking can help identify performance bottlenecks and other issues that may be impacting the performance of the database.
- Evaluating scalability: Benchmarking can be used to evaluate the scalability of the database and identify the maximum number of concurrent connections or transactions that the database can handle without experiencing performance degradation.
- Comparing configurations: Benchmarking can be used to compare the performance of different configurations or systems, such as different hardware or software configurations or different PostgreSQL versions.
- Optimizing queries and indexes: By analyzing the performance metrics obtained from benchmarking, developers and administrators can identify opportunities to

optimize queries, indexes, and other database objects for better performance.
- Validating changes: Benchmarking can be used to validate the performance impact of changes to the database configuration, schema, or workload, such as upgrading to a new PostgreSQL version or adding a new index.

Benchmarking is a critical tool for measuring and evaluating the performance of the PostgreSQL database, as well as identifying and resolving performance bottlenecks and other issues. By regularly benchmarking the database under controlled conditions and analyzing the performance metrics, developers and administrators can optimize the performance and scalability of the PostgreSQL database for better application performance and user experience.

Recipe#2: Benchmark Performance using PGBench

pgbench is a built-in benchmarking tool that comes with PostgreSQL. It is a simple and flexible tool for benchmarking the performance of PostgreSQL databases. In this recipe, I will describe in detail how to use pgbench to benchmark the performance of the adventureworks database.

Connect Adventureworks Database using psql

```
psql -U postgres -d adventureworks
```

Create Test Table for Benchmarking

```
CREATE TABLE test (id serial PRIMARY KEY, data text);
```

This command creates a simple table with an id column and a data column.

Generate Test Data using pgbench

```
pgbench -i -s 10 adventureworks
```

This command generates test data for the adventureworks database, with a scale factor of

10. The scale factor determines the size of the test data, and should be adjusted based on the specific requirements and constraints of your application.

Run Benchmark using pgbench

pgbench -c 10 -j 2 -T 60 -M prepared adventureworks

This command runs a benchmark on the adventureworks database with 10 client connections, 2 threads per client, and a duration of 60 seconds. The -M prepared option specifies that pgbench should use prepared statements, which can improve performance by reducing the overhead of parsing and planning queries.

The benchmark results will be displayed in the console, including the number of transactions per second, the average latency, and other performance metrics.

Use the benchmark results to identify performance bottlenecks and other issues that may be impacting the performance of the database. The following are some key performance metrics to consider:
- Transactions per second: The number of transactions that were processed per second.
- Latency: The average time it took to process each transaction.
- Connection and query throughput: The number of connections and queries that were processed per second.
- Errors and timeouts: The number of errors and timeouts that occurred during the benchmark.

By analyzing these performance metrics, you can identify opportunities to optimize queries, indexes, and other database objects for better performance.

Cleanup Test Data

To clean up the test data and the test table, use the following command:

pgbench -c 1 -j 1 -T 10 -M prepared -n -f cleanup.sql adventureworks

This command runs a cleanup script to remove the test data and the test table from the adventureworks database.

Recipe#3: Responding Error Messages

There are many different types of error messages that can occur while using PostgreSQL database. In this recipe, I will describe some common error messages and how to respond to them using the adventureworks database as an example.

Syntax Error

Syntax errors occur when you enter an invalid command or SQL statement. For example, if you try to run the following SQL statement:

```
SELECT * FROM employee WHERE name = 'John';
```

This will result in a syntax error, because there is no name column in the employee table. To correct this error, you should check the table schema and modify the SQL statement to reference a valid column:

```
SELECT * FROM employee WHERE first_name = 'John';
```

Unique Constraint Violation

Unique constraint violations occur when you try to insert a record with a value that already exists in a unique column. For example, if you try to insert a new employee with a duplicate email address:

```
INSERT INTO employee (first_name, last_name, email) VALUES ('John', 'Doe', 'jdoe@example.com');
```

This will result in a unique constraint violation, because the email address jdoe@example.com already exists in the employee table. To correct this error, you should either update the existing record with the new data or insert a new record with a unique email address.

Insufficient Privileges

Insufficient privileges errors occur when you try to execute a command or SQL statement without the necessary permissions. For example, if you try to create a new table without the CREATE TABLE privilege:

CREATE TABLE sales (id serial PRIMARY KEY, amount numeric);

This will result in an insufficient privileges error. To correct this error, you should grant the necessary privileges to the user or role:

GRANT CREATE TABLE TO myuser;

Connection Refused

Connection refused errors occur when you try to connect to a database but the connection is refused or rejected by the server. For example, if you try to connect to the adventureworks database but the server is not running or is not configured to accept connections:

psql -U postgres -d adventureworks

This will result in a connection refused error. To correct this error, you should check that the server is running and configured correctly, and that the database is accessible over the network.

Server Crashed

Server crashed errors occur when the PostgreSQL server crashes or shuts down unexpectedly. When this happens, you may see an error message like:

FATAL: the database system is in recovery mode

To correct this error, you should try to identify and resolve the cause of the server crash, such as hardware failures, memory leaks, or software bugs. You may also need to perform a database recovery operation to restore the database to a consistent state.

Overall, error messages are a common occurrence when working with PostgreSQL databases. By understanding the different types of error messages and how to respond to them, you can effectively troubleshoot issues and maintain the reliability and availability of the adventureworks database.

Thank You

Epilogue

As we conclude this PostgreSQL 15 Cookbook, we reflect on the many features and capabilities of this powerful relational database management system. Over the course of this book, we have explored a wide range of topics, from basic installation and configuration to advanced query optimization and security.

PostgreSQL 15 offers many new features and enhancements, including improved performance, better support for distributed transactions, and enhanced security features. With these new capabilities, PostgreSQL 15 is even more powerful and reliable than ever before.

As you continue to work with PostgreSQL 15, we hope that this cookbook has served as a helpful guide, providing you with practical solutions to common challenges and inspiring you to explore the many possibilities of this remarkable database system.

We thank you for choosing this cookbook as your guide to PostgreSQL 15, and we hope that it has exceeded your expectations. We encourage you to continue to explore this rich and dynamic ecosystem, and to share your knowledge and experiences with others in the PostgreSQL community.

May your journey with PostgreSQL 15 be a rewarding and fulfilling one, and may you continue to build robust, scalable, and secure applications with this exceptional database system.

Made in the USA
Monee, IL
07 July 2026

56552385R00116